PULPIT HELPS OUT

VOLUME ▶ ONE
TWO
THREE
FOUR

NEW TESTAMENT
SERMON STARTERS

*A Full Year's Worth of Dynamic Word Study Outlines
to Jumpstart your Preaching, Teaching, and Personal Study*

SPIROS ZODHIATES

AMG Publishers

52 New Testament Sermon Starters
Volume Three

© 2001 by Spiros Zodhiates
All Rights Reserved.

Formerly Published as *Exegetical Preaching, Volume Three*

ISBN 0–89957–487–4

Printed in the United States of America
05 04 03 02   –R– 6 5 4 3

CONTENTS

Preface		ix
1. The Temptation of Jesus	Matt. 4:1–11	1
2. Sowing the Seed	Matt. 13:1–9	3
3. Why Did Jesus Call Fishermen to Be His Disciples?	Mark 1:14–20	5
4. Jesus, Master of the Storm	Mark 4:35–41	9
5. He Who Made the Physical Laws Can Bypass Them	Mark 6:45–52	12
6. God's Law or Man's Tradition?	Mark 7:1–8	15
7. The Transfiguration of Our Lord	Mark 9:2–9	18
8. The First Shall Be Last	Mark 9:30–37	21
9. Why Jesus Entered Jerusalem Triumphantly	Mark 11:1–11	24
10. John the Baptist—His Call and Ministry	Luke 3:1–6	27
11. Covetousness	Luke 12:15	31
12. Leprosy Symbolizes Sin	Luke 17:11	33
13. How to Be Fully Satisfied Here and Now	Luke 14:16–24	36
14. "Look Up"	Luke 21:25–36	39
15. The Incarnation of God the Son	John 1:1–18	42
16. Easy Religion	John 2:13–22	45
17. Cultured But Not Born Again	John 3:1–17	48
18. What the Cross and Resurrection Can Do for You	John 3:14–21	50
19. Jesus Before Pilate	John 18:33–37	54
20. How We Are Justified Before God	Rom. 4:1–5	57
21. What Is Justification?	Rom. 5:1–5	61
22. The Results of Our Justification	Rom. 5:1–11	65
23. The Believer's Conflict with Sin	Rom. 7:14–25	70
24. Who Cannot Please God?	Rom. 8:8	73
25. How You Can Be Saved	Rom. 10:8–13	77
26. Man's Responsibility Toward God	Rom. 12:1–13	79

Contents

27. The Prudent Use of Our Liberty in Christ	Rom. 14:1–23	82
28. Should All Christians Agree on Everything?	1 Cor. 1:1–17	85
29. Two Kinds of Christians	1 Cor. 3:1–9	90
30. The Purpose of Pentecost	1 Cor. 12:3–13	94
31. What Guarantee Do We Have That We Shall Be Raised from the Dead?	1 Cor. 15:2–28	97
32. How to Be Reconciled to God	2 Cor. 5:16–21	100
33. The Blessing of Suffering	Phil. 3:8–14	104
34. How to Be an Example Worth Following	Phil. 3:17—4:1	108
35. The Resources and Responsibilities of the Believer	Col. 1:9–11	113
36. What Is Reconciliation?	Col. 1:20–29	115
37. Spiritual Garments Befitting the Christian	Col. 3:12–17	117
38. Paul's Work Among the Thessalonians Was Short but Effective	1 Thess. 2:1–8	121
39. When Is Church Discipline Necessary?	2 Thess. 3:6–13	124
40. For What and for Whom Should a Christian Pray?	1 Tim. 2:1–8	126
41. Paul's Thoughts Just Before His Death	2 Tim. 1:1–14	130
42. Preaching That Soothes the Audience	2 Tim. 3:14; 4:5	134
43. Philemon and a Returned Wayward Slave, Onesimus	Phile. 1:1–12	137
44. Faith as a Conductor of Invaluable Knowledge	Heb. 11:1–3	141
45. Cure for Christian Weariness	Heb. 12:1, 2	144
46. Two Mountains Contrasted	Heb. 12:18–29	146
47. Principles of Christian Conduct	Heb. 13:1–5	148
48. The Hope Born of the Resurrection of Christ	1 Pet. 1:3–9	151

Contents

49. Desire Health Food, Discard Junk Food, and Grow Up	1 Pet. 2:2–10	154
50. God's Word and the Splitting of the Atom	2 Pet. 3:8–14	158
51. The Eternal God	Rev. 1:1–4	161
52. The State of Christian Believers	Rev. 21:1–6	163
Index of Greek Words		165
Scripture Index		187

PREFACE

This book is a compilation of selected outlines which previously have been published in "Pulpit and Bible Study Helps," a publication used by over 200,000 pastors and teachers of the Bible. These outlines are written to meet the need of those who follow the Lectionary, a system used by a number of churches. Each outline follows in order from Matthew to Revelation, one for every week of the year.

The unique features of this book include a key verse given for each outline, which is the focus of the entire passage the outline covers. In addition, an Index of Greek Words is provided listing each Greek word (transliterated) mentioned in the outlines along with a definition, the Scripture references where the word is found (if applicable), and the page number where each word occurs.

My prayer is that this volume of outlines will serve to be beneficial to those of you who are involved in teaching and preaching God's Word.

Spiros Zodhiates

The Temptation of Jesus

Key Verses: Matthew 4:1-11

I. The Meaning of the Words "Tempt" and "Temptation"
   A. The two Greek words are the verb *peirázo* and the noun *peirasmós*. They derive from the root word *peíra* which means "experience, trial," which in turn derives from the verb *peirõ*, "to perforate, pierce through" in order to find out the constitution of someone or something. If steel is going to be used for a building, its constitution must be tried to see whether it is strong enough for the job destined for it.
   B. The devil tempts us with the express purpose of showing that we are failures. His main effort is to destroy the trust we have in God and His Christ.
   C. God never tempts us in that way. He tries us to prove to us and others that we can be used and promoted with greater trust by Him. Therefore, the meaning of the word depends on who uses it.

II. Jesus Allows Himself to Be Tempted To:
   A. Prove to us that there is a devil and that he is active in the world. In fact, Paul calls him "the prince of the power of the air" (Eph. 2:2). If there is no devil, then Jesus was a liar or was personally deceived.
   B. Prove to us that since the devil tempted even Jesus, there is not a single one of us he will leave alone.
   C. Teach us that as He faced the devil victoriously, so can we with His Word and His power.
   D. Show us that whatever is suggested by the devil cannot possibly be for our eternal good.

E. Show us that giving priority to material prosperity, symbolized by the making of bread out of stones and premature fame, by ruling over the kingdoms of the world, are of the devil. God never desires that we have material prosperity at the expense of our inner, spiritual relationship with Him. It must be God's kingdom and righteousness first, and then all our physical needs (Matt. 6:33).
   F. Show us that out of every temptation of the devil we can become stronger; then Jesus will entrust us with greater responsibilities in His kingdom.

III. Christ Taught Us to Pray, "Lead Us Not into Temptation" To:
   A. Show us how easily we can misunderstand God's purposes in the experiences and situations He permits in our lives. What we think to be temptation can actually be exercise for acquiring strength. "Count it all joy when ye shall fall into divers temptations" (James 1:2). Let us recognize God's hand of strengthening and training in what we would rather shun.
   B. Show us that where God leads us, He does not abandon us, but walks with us (Ps. 23:4).

Sowing the Seed

Key Verses: Matthew 13:1-9

I. The Sowing of the Seed
   A. God's Word is being continually scattered abroad.
      1. In this parable, Jesus states, "Behold, a sower went forth to sow" (Matt. 13:3). The exact translation is, "He came out, the sowing one [a participial noun, *ho speírōn*], to sow continuously [*toú speírein*, the present infinitive of *speírō*, to sow, scatter]."
      2. In verse 4, a literal translation of the opening clause is, "and in the process of his sowing [*en tṓ speírein autón*]."
      3. All these verbs are in the present, indicating a continuity in the process.
   B. It falls upon diverse plots of ground.

II. Hindrances to the Seed
   A. The fowls that came and devoured the seed represent the devil, who is said to be "the prince of the power of the air" (Eph. 2:2). Jesus explained it thus: "When any one heareth the word of the kingdom, and understandeth it not, then cometh the wicked one, and catcheth away that which was sown in his heart" (Matt. 13:19).
   B. The "stony places, where they had not much earth," denote a slick superficiality which seeks instant joy without counting the cost (Matt. 13:5, 20). Then "when tribulation or persecution ariseth because of the word, by and by he is offended" (Matt. 13:21).
   C. Finally, the "thorns" that spring up and choke the seeds are selfish anxiety and "the deceitfulness of

riches" (Matt. 13:7, 22). We are so anxious to succeed in this world that we fail to heed the Word of God.

III. **The Growth of the Seed**
   A. God will always insure that there is some good ground wherein the seed can take root (Is. 55:10, 11).
   B. The growth of the seed is supernaturally directed by God, as seen in the parable found in Mark 4:26–29.
   C. The fruit that results occurs not at one time only, but continuously, as indicated by the imperfect tense of the verb *edídou*, "was giving or bringing forth" (not "brought forth" as the KJV has it). Salvation yields a constant supply of spiritual fruit: "love, joy, peace, longsuffering, gentleness, goodness, faith, meekness, temperance . . ." (Gal. 5:22).
   D. There are also degrees of productivity, ". . . some a hundredfold, some sixtyfold, some thirtyfold" (Matt. 13:23). In the body of Christ, not all possess the same gifts (1 Cor. 12:11), but each is to yield an increase with the talents he has been given (Matt. 25:27).

Why Did Jesus Call Fishermen to Be His Disciples?

Key Verses: Mark 1:14-20

I. Jesus Acted Contrary to Human Expectations
  A. He did not choose the learned and the humanly wise.
    1. The wise of this earth were too proud of their knowledge. It is far more difficult to build where there is already a structure.
    2. He knew they would call the gospel "foolishness" (1 Cor. 1:23). How could Christ persuade the intelligentsia that they would have to put aside the power they exercised in order to show love? (1 Cor. 13:8).
    3. He knew that pride and power are the two greatest obstacles to believing the kingdom of God would not come into being through merely understanding it nor through a violent imposition of it. The Lord Jesus' message was simple but unalterable: "repent and believe the gospel" (Mark 1:15).
  B. He did not choose the rich and those of high position.
    1. An overabundance of material possessions may lead to drunkenness, debauchery and an incapacity to know what one truly is. Success is misconceived as sufficient, but often proves disastrous in the end (Matt. 19:23, 24; Luke 12:13–21).
    2. One's possessions become such a part of him that it is hard to see there is something better for which it is worthwhile to sacrifice (Luke 18:18–23).

C. Christ did not choose the religionists.
1. One would think that the temple or the synagogue would have been the place where Jesus would have gone to select His disciples. After all, that is where the pious were supposed to be.
2. The Lord knew that their traditional piety was neither genuine nor true. To them the most important thing was not God's Word as originally given, but "the traditions of the elders" (Matt. 15:2, 3, 6; Mark 7:3–13). Even today it is easier to bring one to Christ who has never heard of Him than one who is wrapped up in a false "Christian" tradition.

D. Christ did not choose the politicians.
1. They were polarized. If He had chosen political leaders from among the Romans, the Jews would be excluded; and if from among the Jews, the Romans and Gentiles would be excluded.
2. The Lord's main concern was to give the immediate understanding that the gospel He came to bring and preach was for everybody, for the whole world, although the first opportunity was given to the Jews (Matt. 1:21; John 1:11, 12; 3:16; 1 John 2:2).

II. **But Why Fishermen?**
A. Because of the contempt and neglect those fishermen experienced in their lives, who would ever choose a fisherman for leadership? He wanted to prove that "the foolishness of God is wiser than men; and the weakness of God is stronger than men" (1 Cor. 1:25, 27). He wanted to show that God can use anybody if he or she will simply make themselves available.
B. Jesus calls not those on whom He can build, but those for whom He can become the very foundation of their lives. The greatest misunderstanding of the principle of the Lord is that He wants what we think we are and

what we have in order to build on it. His building must not be built on a human foundation. **He** must be the foundation (1 Cor. 3:10–12). Jesus does not want us because of what we are and what we have, but He wants us for what He can make of us. Observe what He said in verse 17: "Come ye after me, and I will make you **to become** fishers of men." This involves:
1. Our willingness to come and leave everything behind.
2. Our building a superstructure on the foundation He has laid (1 Cor. 3:10–15). To become a fisherman depends basically on the Lord as far as the foundation is concerned, but it also depends on how we build on it.

III. The Common Characteristics of Fishermen of Fish and of Souls

A. They work together with others. These fishermen were not lonely individuals who would bait a line and fish for one at a time. If we want to catch more than one fish at a time, as we indeed should in the tradition of Andrew and Philip, we must learn to cooperate with others.

B. The net that Peter and Andrew were casting was called *amphíblēstron* (Matt. 4:18), literally a net that one would cast in the water over the shoulder and which would spread in a circle, sinking as a result of the weights and then be pulled in with fish in it. The word derives from *amphí,* "around," and *bállō,* "cast, throw." That is a perfect simile of how we should be catching men. A line with a hook deceives the fish by thinking it is food and catches it struggling for life, soon to die. The net catches them alive. To catch men alive, we must put out arms of love around them, not stick hooks in their mouths.

C. A fisherman separates the fish he catches, attributing value to them. He takes to the market place only the edible ones. One of the gifts of the Spirit is "discernings" (*diakríseis* in the plural) of spirits (1 Cor. 12:10). A mature Christian is one who can discern between the good and the bad fish he catches (Heb. 5:14).
D. A fisherman is a hard worker. He is not a bureaucrat. How wonderful if bureaucrats kept out of the ministry. Jesus did not call people who had nothing to do. He called ambitious people who loved to be busy, for God's work is no easy path.

Jesus, Master of the Storm

Key Verses: Mark 4:35–41

I. When Did This Event Take Place?
   A. Mark 4:35 defines the time as "the same day, when the even was come. . . ." It was in the evening or late afternoon of the day on which the Lord had spoken from the boat of one of His disciples and given the Parable of the Sower and others associated with it. He and His followers then set out from the neighborhood of Capernaum to cross the Lake of Galilee to its eastern shore.
   B. Matthew and Luke connect it with many other incidents because they do not follow chronological order as does Mark. Thus, Matthew places the crossing immediately before the account of the three men who wanted to become His followers (Matt. 8:19–26), and Luke, after the incident of Jesus' relatives coming to see Him (Luke 8:19–25).
   C. The Lord must have been physically exhausted after teaching all day. Therefore, as soon as they set sail, He went to the back part of the ship and fell asleep. Because of His humanity, He also needed sleep after a day of hard work.
   D. He did not take time to change clothes; the disciples "took Him even as He was in the ship" (Mark 4:36). Apparently He found the only pillow (*tó proskephálaion*, the pillow) and went right to sleep.

II. Why Did the Storm Arise?

A. It was Jesus who said, "Let us pass over unto the other side" (Mark 4:35), and His disciples readily obeyed Him.

B. Storms arise not only as a consequence of our sin, but also as a result of our obedience. Such tribulation produces glory rather than shame, as Romans 8:17 clearly states, "If so be that we suffer with Him [Christ], that we may be also glorified together."

C. Christ also shared in the same storm as His disciples. "For we have not a high priest which cannot be touched with the feeling of our infirmities; but was in all points tempted like as we are, yet without sin" (Heb. 4:15). If we suffer for obeying Christ, He will be right there with us in the midst of the storm.

III. The Storm Was Unexpected

A. They departed in the calm of the evening. Because the sea of Galilee is surrounded by the Golan heights and other hills, sudden winds can arise producing great waves. Certainly, had they known it was going to be so rough, they would have waited until the storm was over before crossing.

B. When the storm did arise, the disciples tried to battle it with their human skill.

C. They expected Jesus to help them before they requested His assistance. But His greatest demonstrations of power often occur when He delays in intervening. For example, when He heard that His friend Lazarus was sick, He waited until he died, so that an even greater miracle could be performed: raising him from the dead. In this instance, the Lord continued to sleep in order that they might see His complete power over the forces of nature.

D. Very few people will acknowledge that they are not sufficient in themselves to handle the storms of life.

To absolve themselves, they do not hesitate to blame the indifference of others as the causes of their suffering. How the Lord must have hurt when His disciples said to Him, "Master [teacher, *didáskale*] carest thou not that we perish?" (v. 38). They should have said, "Lord, help us for we cannot help ourselves." When they did come to this point, then the Lord was ready to calm the storm.

IV. Jesus Demonstrated His Deity
   A. First Jesus awoke. The word in verse 38 translated "and they awake Him" is *diegeírousin*. In verse 39 the same verb in the passive participle, *diegertheís*, is translated "and He arose." The verb *diegeírō* derives from *diá*, an intensive meaning "completely" and *egeírō*, "to rise." It indicates the shock of waking suddenly from sleep.
   B. He did not at first chide the disciples for being terrified. Instead, he "rebuked the wind," and calmed the sea (v. 39). There was no mistaking that the storm stopped in response to His command.
   C. Then He addressed the disciples with the questions: "Why are ye so fearful" or timid (*deiloí*)? "How is it that ye have no faith?" (v. 40). He was referring to their fear of the storm.
   D. It was after Jesus had calmed the waves that they became afraid (*ephobḗthēsan*) "exceedingly" (v. 41). Instead of being reassured and thanking Jesus, they began discussing with each other *tís ára hoútos estin*, "What manner of man is this; that even the wind and the sea obey Him?" (v. 41). They suddenly had glimpsed the deity of Christ and that "in him dwelleth all the fullness of the Godhead bodily" (Col. 2:9).

He Who Made the Physical Laws Can Bypass Them

Key Verses: Mark 6:45-52

I. They Wanted to Make Him King
   A. After miraculously feeding the 5,000 Jesus could see that the populace intended to make Him king by force (John 6:15).
   B. They did not realize that His First Coming was for the purpose of establishing His spiritual kingdom in their hearts (Luke 17:20, 21) rather than political freedom for Israel.
   C. Their subjugation to the Romans was not as disabling as their sin.
   D. Their desire to humanly elevate Him to kingship was exactly the opposite of what He had come to accomplish. He had come to bear the cross, not to wear the crown.
   E. Unfortunately, the disciples also entertained self-aggrandizing ideas of power (Matt. 20:20–28; Mark 10:35–45).
   F. Upon this occasion, Mark records that Jesus had to actually force the disciples to get into the boat and sail to the other side of the lake while He dismissed the crowds and went to a nearby mountain to pray (Mark 6:45, 46).

II. The Apostles Made Slow Progress Until Jesus' Sudden Appearance

A. Although the disciples rowed for nine hours, they hardly managed to go two miles distance because of the wind.

B. The believer's progress may well be much slower and rougher when he is forced by His Lord to proceed in a certain path.

C. Jesus, however, was following the scene with His far-reaching eye. He never loses sight of a disciple in a storm.

D. He then decided to intervene when least expected and in a humanly impossible way, by walking to them on the water.

E. When they saw Him, they thought He was a phantom, and instead of being comforted, they were afraid.
   1. When the angel appeared to Zacharias to tell him about Elizabeth's son, Zacharias was afraid (Luke 1:11, 12).
   2. Mary, likewise, feared the appearance of a supernatural being (Luke 1:30).
   3. The angel also told the shepherds to "Fear not" when he came upon them in the fields around Bethlehem (Luke 2:10).

III. This Miracle Is Proof of Christ's Deity

A. Man can make a boat that will sail on water, but only God can walk on the water by his own power.

B. John 1:3 declares that "All things were made by him; and without him was not anything made that was made." Jesus Himself is creator of the universe.

C. It was therefore easy for Him to bypass His own laws of nature at will. Jesus, being God (Col. 2:9), could walk on water as easily as on solid ground.

IV. Why Did the Lord Permit the Storm?
  A. The disciples agreed with the crowd who wanted to acclaim Jesus as a human king. He sent them into a storm to focus their attention on spiritual reality.
  B. Jesus separated Himself from the disciples temporarily to show them what would happen after He had ascended into heaven. Our encounters with early difficulties fit us for later service.
  C. Moreover, the disciples were ready to receive His supernatural aid after their human attempts proved futile. Jesus gave them time to see their own helplessness.
  D. The waves signify our difficulties which Jesus uses as the means to teach us. Our trials then become His avenue to our hearts.
  E. Unrecognized, Jesus brings fear; but recognized, He brings relief.

God's Law or Man's Tradition?

Key Verses: Mark 7:1-8, 14, 15

I. Jesus' Enemies Gathered Against Him
   A. In Mark 6:30, Jesus' apostles "gathered themselves together unto Jesus." The Greek word, *sunágontai*, is correctly rendered "gathered themselves together."
   B. In Mark 7:1 the same Greek verb is used to describe the assembling of His adversaries, the Pharisees and scribes who came as a delegation from Jerusalem to discredit Him.

II. Two Opposing Ideals Clash
   A. Jesus taught that the disposition of the heart toward God was the most important matter.
   B. His enemies believed, on the other hand, in the external compliance with tradition, whether or not it conformed to God's teaching (Mark 7:6, 13).
   C. Thus, when Jesus' enemies saw that His disciples were eating with unwashed hands, they faulted them, not because of hygienic reasons, but because it was contrary to "the tradition of the elders" (Matt. 15:2; Mark 7:2, 3).

III. What Is Tradition?
   A. The Greek word for tradition is *parádosis*, which means transmission from (*pará*) one to another until something becomes a way of life. *Parádosis*, as indicated in Matthew 15:2, 3, 6 and Mark 7:3, 5, 8, 9, 13 shows that an idea may become accepted without due

examination of its correctness as measured against an absolute standard. For instance, a merchant might call a weight of 15 ounces a pound. Soon others adopt it as a pound even though it is still only 15 ounces. Since the new measurement suits the interest of many, it becomes accepted as true.

B. In contrast to tradition is "the command of God" (Matt. 15:3, 6) also called "the word of God" (Mark 7:13). Jesus taught that the commandments of God are the standard by which to determine if a tradition is valid and should be followed.

C. Human tendency has always been to reduce God's laws to certain external acts which can be obeyed without a true change of heart taking place. When others saw the Pharisees wash their hands before a meal, they took it for granted that they also possessed a clean heart, which was not necessarily so. Jesus called such hypocrisy outward parading of righteousness (Matt. 6:2, 5, 16; 23:13–15; Mark 7:6).

IV. How Did the Jewish Traditions Originate?

A. These traditions began with a wrong interpretation of Exodus 20:1: "And God spake all these words, saying. . . ." Instead of sticking with the ten written commandments given to Moses as their standard, the rabbis extrapolated 613 "spoken" commandments to be followed as well.

B. These "spoken" commandments were codified and strictly adhered to by the Pharisees. The scribes examined both the written Word of God and the traditions, while the Sadducees were the intellectual questioners of their day.

C. Jesus, on the other hand, actually reduced the ten written commandments to two (Matt. 22:37–40), which stressed inward devotion as primary.

D. He referred to Jewish traditions as being from the elders and not Moses because they were not the inspired Word of God.

V. Jesus Used the Example of Corban (Mark 7:9–13) to Illustrate Their Error

A. Corban was an offering promised to God. Unfortunately, many used it as a way to avoid filial responsibility. Since the money had already been offered to God, they reasoned it could not be used to support their parents. This tradition contradicted the explicitly written fifth commandment, "Honor thy father and thy mother" (Ex. 20:12) and should not have been followed.

B. Jesus taught that one who puts God first in his life, following "the first and great commandment" (Matt. 22:37, 38), will then put relatives and possessions in their proper place. The child who loves Jesus above all will certainly use his possessions to care for his parents. Our love of the Lord will thus lead us to fulfill the second great commandment, "love thy neighbor as thyself" (Matt. 22:39).

VI. Likewise Today, Church Traditions Are Not to Be Followed Blindly

A. Since the advent of Christ's church, certain traditions, both good and bad, have developed.

B. It behooves every individual to examine them in light of the written Word of God. If they can be supported by it without reducing spiritual life to mere formalism, then they may be observed.

C. The rule which Christ set down in Mark 7:8 is relevant today. We must not lay aside the commandment of God in order to hold to the tradition of men. The Scriptures, not church traditions, are to be our final authority.

The Transfiguration of Our Lord

Key Verses: Mark 9:2-9

I. Peter, James and John with Jesus on the Mountain
   A. Jesus took the three leading disciples so that they might see one of the most extraordinary events permissible on earth.
   B. He could have described the event to them, but they would not possibly be able to understand, being in an earthly body.
   C. Whenever the Lord wanted to pray in strict communication between Himself and His Father, He prayed in solitude (Mark 1:35; 6:46; Luke 5:16; 6:12; 9:18).
   D. The Lord prayed in public only when He wanted to reveal certain truths to others (Matt. 11:25; Luke 3:21; John 11:41; 17:1).

II. The Events on the Mount of Transfiguration
   A. The noun "transfiguration" (*metamórphōsis*) never occurs in the New Testament, but the verb *metamorphó* or *metamorphoúmai* in the middle voice occurs four times.
   B. In Matthew 17:2 and Mark 9:2, *metamorphoúmai* is used in connection with the physical body of Jesus on the mountain, which probably was Mt. Hermon, being the highest in the area, about 9,000 feet above sea level (Matt. 17:1; Mark 9:2). In Romans 12:2 and 2 Corinthians 3:18 the word is used in a figurative sense meaning "transform" or "change."

C. The verb *metamorphó*, "to transfigure," is made up of the preposition *metá*, denoting change of condition, and *morphó*, found only in the passive form (*morphoúmai* in Galatians 4:19, "until Christ be formed in you"). The substantive *morphé*, "form," has great theological importance in relation to the person of Christ in His post-resurrection appearance to the Emmaus disciples (Mark 16:12) and His incarnation (Phil. 2:6, 7), especially as it relates to *schéma*, "shape."

D. The word does not simply mean that the disciples saw an illusion or a fantasy. Jesus Christ's body changed into a new form, *morphé*, in substance and appearance, not merely *schéma*, the outward figure, in which case the word *metaschematízō* (1 Cor. 4:6; 2 Cor. 11:13–15; Phil. 3:21) would have been used.

E. In Luke 9:28–36 where this event is recorded, the verb is not *metamorphó*, "to transfigure," but the expression "the fashion of his countenance was altered" (Luke 9:29). The Greek is *eídos*, the object of sight, the appearance of His face and *héteron*, "another," different from the previous. Jesus became, *egéneto*, a person with a face different than He had before in the presence of the disciples.

F. Jesus, therefore, became in essence and appearance what He was not in His earthly body. We are helped to understand this by the use of the expression "in another form" in Mark 16:12 referring to the risen Jesus' appearance to the two disciples from Emmaus. The Greek is *en hetéra morphé*, "in a qualitatively different essence and appearance." That is the meaning of *metamorphó*, "to transfigure." It was a temporary change of Jesus' body to that which it would be after His resurrection.

III. The Lessons of the Transfiguration

A. Jesus could change His essence and appearance at will in full demonstration of His deity, showing that the fullness of the Godhead dwelt in Him bodily (Col. 2:9).

B. He wanted to let the disciples have a foretaste of the glory of the resurrection. The Lord never referred to His cross without also referring to the resurrection.

C. The appearance of Moses and Elijah proved they were still in existence and they appeared fully recognizable. There is no extinction or sleep after death as far as the real personality, the spirit, is concerned.

D. Moses represented the law and Elijah the prophets, both being fulfilled and finding their culmination in the person of Jesus Christ.

The First Shall Be Last

Key Verses: Mark 9:30–37

I. What Preceded the Unfortunate Subject of the Disciples' Conversation on Their Return to Capernaum?
   A. Jesus had begun to teach His disciples about His cross and resurrection. Mark 9:32 reveals their attitude concerning Christ's future suffering: "But they understood not that saying, and were afraid to ask him." The verb for "understood not" is *ēgnóoun*, the imperfect of *agnoéō*, which may refer to voluntary ignorance. I prefer to translate it, "and they ignored the utterance." They dismissed it because it was too painful to contemplate. They obviously understood what Jesus was saying because He could not have made it any plainer. Like Peter's earlier response (Mark 8:32), they too objected and wanted to hear no more about suffering and death.
   B. Instead, they consoled themselves with thoughts of the coming kingdom and their position in it.

II. Jesus Took the Initiative to Ask Them What They Were Talking About
   A. They hadn't shared their speculations with Jesus.
   B. Jesus therefore asked them, "What was it that ye disputed among yourselves by the way?" (Mark 9:33). The Greek verb for "disputed" is *dielogízesthe*, which actually means "were figuring out in one's mind." Having ignored unpleasant reality, they preferred to daydream about their own importance or "who should be the greatest" (Mark 9:34). Such was their irresponsibility!

III. The Disciples Are Embarrassed

A. "But they held their peace" (Mark 9:34) is a euphemistic translation of the Greek word *esiōpōn*, they were keeping silent. What could they answer? How will we answer at a future time when all the thoughts of our hearts are revealed?

B. Luke 9:47 says, "And Jesus, perceiving the thought of their heart." The word for thought is *dialogismós*, also translated reasoning (Luke 9:46). Jesus saw their thoughts. He judges not only our actions but also our thoughts (Matt. 5:28, 29).

C. Although they numbered at least twelve, Luke 9:47 does not speak of the thoughts of their hearts, but of the thought of their one heart. When it comes to ambition, what a unanimity of thought there is!

D. Then Jesus sat down and called the twelve. The following lecture left no doubt that He knew their hearts.

IV. Jesus Rebuked Them Constructively

A. He did not comment on their selfishness.

B. Instead, He instructed them on how to become the first in the kingdom, "If any man desire to be first, the same shall be last of all, and servant of all" (Mark 9:35).

C. What inferences can be made from this precept?
  1. Ambition is not bad by itself.
  2. Wishful thinking will not make one first.
  3. We must be willing to start and finish at the bottom of the ladder.
  4. Elevation is achieved by considering oneself as a servant of all.
  5. Nobody can truly find joy in life who does not find others whom he can serve.

D. Jesus then stood a child in their midst as an object lesson, saying, "Whosoever shall receive one of such chil-

dren in My name, receiveth Me; and whosoever shall receive Me, receiveth not Me, but Him that sent Me" (Mark 9:37).
1. A child represents weakness and helplessness.
2. One serves Christ by serving the weak and the helpless.
3. By serving Jesus, one serves God the Father.

Why Jesus Entered Jerusalem Triumphantly

Key Verses: Mark 11:1–11

I. The Event Was So Important That It Was Recorded by All Four Evangelists
   Matt. 21:1–11; Mark 11:1–11; Luke 19:28–40; John 12:12–19

II. It Was Not an Experiment for the Purpose of Avoiding Death
   A. He was not offering Himself for the last time to Israel as her King.
   B. He had announced at the outset that all should "Repent: for the kingdom of heaven is at hand" (Matt. 4:17).
      1. However, this was not an external kingdom He was going to establish, but an internal one in the hearts of those who would repent.
      2. Jesus taught that there were two kingdoms, one spiritual which was immediate and individual, and one physical which was going to be accomplished at His Second Coming and which concerns Israel as a nation and all those who would repent and accept His spiritual kingship in their hearts (See Luke 17:20–24).
   C. To show that He was indeed capable of accomplishing His triumphant entrance into Jerusalem and the world at His Second Coming "on His day" (Luke 17:24; Matt. 25:31–36), He entered on the Sunday before His resurrection as He was about to deliver himself to die by the hands of His enemies.

Why Jesus Entered Jerusalem Triumphantly

D. Palm Sunday was a deliberate demonstration of what Jesus was capable of doing in the long run for those who would receive Him as their Lord and Savior during the dispensation of His grace.

III. **Jesus Was Going to Deliver Himself as a Lamb to Be Slain, but He Was Also the King Who Was Yet to Come**
   A. To make this believable, He caused the silence of His enemies on Palm Sunday. Not a word or a single act of opposition was indicated as the whole city, with some three million celebrants, roared out a thunderous, unanimous welcome, "Hosanna, blessed is He that cometh in the name of the Lord."
   B. They all misunderstood His actions.
      1. The disciples thought that since He had power over death, having already raised a boy (Luke 7:11–16), a girl (Luke 8:49–55), and Lazarus (John 11:38–44), He would not die. But He came to die (John 1:29; 12:27) and He would not give up the purpose for which He came simply because He was acclaimed and welcomed in Jerusalem. He did not come the first time for corporate acceptance (John 1:11) but for individual reception into the hearts of people. He came to reconcile the enemies of God the Father, and this could only be accomplished through the shedding of His blood to satisfy God's justice for the sin of mankind and to change the sinner into a saint (2 Cor. 5:15, 17, 21).
      2. His enemies were dumbfounded. They kept silent not because they finally accepted His teaching and purpose, but because of the fear which this demonstration of acceptance produced. They must have thought to themselves thus: "If this Man really has such power and we are unable to kill Him and He truly imposes His kingdom upon us, what will happen to us if we resist? It is safer to shout Hosanna

with His friends than to oppose Him." This rationalization kept them silent, until they realized that Jesus, on His own, was not going to capitalize on this demonstration of power. He quit the triumphant demonstration as quickly and as voluntarily as He started it. He could have ruled if He had chosen to, but He came the first time not to rule but to save (Matt. 1:21; 18:11)—though He said and was now demonstrating He could indeed come back to rule.

IV. **The Triumphant Entry Was Initiated, Planned, and Executed by Jesus Himself**
   A. He knew what the Scriptures prophesied (Zech. 9:9, 10) and He fulfilled them exactly in a climate of unbelievable hatred against Him.
   B. He borrowed a colt which had never been ridden by anyone.
   C. He told His disciples where to find it and what to say to its owner. Thus He imposed His will, as He will again upon His enemies when He returns (1 Cor. 15:24–28; 2 Thess. 1:7–10). As on Palm Sunday, so also at His Second Coming there will be His friends and His enemies, and His plan will be executed voluntarily by His own and involuntarily by His enemies.
   D. He did not send an advance publicity team, nor did He deliver a persuasive speech. He simply entered, deliberately in full command and in absolute triumph, into an atmosphere that was against Him. Absolute power was demonstrated by a man riding on a donkey! Unbelievable, but as it became history, so prophecy of His Second Coming will become history.

John the Baptist—His Call and Ministry

Key Verses: Luke 3:1-6

I. **Christianity Is Not a Figment of the Imagination, But a Historical Fact**
   A. Christianity is not an idea, a philosophy, but is a historical person called Jesus Christ.
   B. When John the Baptist appeared on the scene as the forerunner of Jesus, he was placed in a historical context, given to us in Luke 3:1, 2.
   C. Four secular rulers are mentioned whose chronological, geographical and functional contexts are set. They are:
      1. Pontius Pilate, who ruled in Judea and whose likeness one can see in a plaque at the entrance of Caesarea Maritime, from where he ruled.
      2. Herod who ruled Galilee.
      3. Philip, Herod's brother who ruled Ituraea and Trachonites (northwest of Damascus).
      4. Lysanias, the ruler (tetrarch, ruler along with three others, making the fourth ruler) of Abilene.
   D. In addition, Luke names two religious rulers of that day (Luke 3:2).
      1. Annas was appointed high priest in A.D. 6 and deposed in A.D. 15. In spite of his overthrow by the Romans, the Jews considered him high priest for life. He ruled with his son-in-law, Caiaphas, at the time of John the Baptist.
      2. Caiaphas also officiated later at the trial of Jesus, with Annas carrying on the preliminary investigation (John 18:13–24). In Luke 3:2 the word "high

priest" is in the singular followed by the two names of Annas and Caiaphas—deliberately so stated to indicate that although Caiaphas was the high priest officially appointed by Rome, his father-in-law shared his high-priestly power.

II. It Was into Such a Setting That John the Baptist Came Out of Obscurity (Luke. 3:2)
A. John was the son of a priest.
B. He was living in the wilderness at the time of his call.
C. He was not propelled by his saintly parents, thinking that God who gave him to them at such an advanced age must have something important for him to do.
D. They waited upon the Lord for the proper time and the revealed task. Any earlier projection by the parents would have missed God's purpose.
E. Human ambition usually misses God's specific calling.
F. John was willing to wait in the desert for God's time.

III. The Influence of the Family
A. He is named in association with his father Zacharias. This indicates how important is the family in the role it plays in the preparation of anyone's character and vocation.
B. His family was satisfied in the social and economic lot in which God permitted them to be. Luke 1:80 is important: "And the child grew, and waxed strong in spirit, and was in the deserts till the day of his showing unto Israel."
C. His parents placed John's spiritual growth above all else. (It is a great mistake of parents today to neglect their children's spiritual development.)
D. The word that is translated "grew" in Greek is *eúxane*, the imperfect of *auxánō,* to grow with an influence outside oneself. That is the verb used in 1 Cor. 3:6: "I

have planted, Apollos watered, but God gave the increase (*eúxanen*). This means that without God having incorporated into the seed the element of life, it could not grow simply through human endeavor. So it was with John as a child. His spiritual growth was due to his godly parents.

E. The verb *eúxane* in Luke 1:80 is in the imperfect, which refers to the constant influence his parents brought about in his spiritual growth.

F. What is translated "waxed strong" is *ekrataioúto*, the imperfect passive of *krataióō*, to make strong. He was made strong. The word is also used in Luke 2:40; Ephesians 3:16; 1 Cor. 16:13. The principle word *krátos* refers more to stability and steadfastness of strength than to mere physical strength. This also was constantly done by his parents. John was helped by his parents to become a stable character.

G. Premature debut can be disastrous. ". . . and was in the deserts till the day of his showing unto Israel" (Luke 1:80). John waited for "the day." He did not become anxious. He was six months older than Jesus. He did not appear on the scene of action till he was over thirty years old. It took that many years of preparation and waiting till "the day" came.

H. ". . . till the day of his showing unto Israel" (Luke 1:80). The word translated "showing" is *anádeixis*, which has the meaning of public propulsion. The verb *anadeíknumi*, to show by raising high or aloft, is used in Luke 10:1 where it means to publicly show. John the Baptist stayed hidden in the deserts waiting for the day of his public propulsion by God Himself. Oh, that we might all have the patience to wait for that momentous day in our lives!

IV. At Last, God Spoke to John ". . . the word of God came unto John the son of Zacharias" (Luke 3:2)
   A. Despite his auspicious birth, John had to wait until God's call came to him.
   B. God will invariably direct the one who is prepared spiritually to serve Him.
   C. The Greek word translated "word" is *rhēma*, utterance. There are actually two Greek words which are translated "word." The other Greek word is *lógos* which is sometimes used for the whole message, while *rhēma* refers to an isolated specific affirmation, especially in the prophetical writings. This seems to fit in the case of John. God revealed to John what He wanted him to do in particular. For instance, Jesus is called the Word, *Lógos*, because He is God's total revelation to the world (John 1:1).

V. John Obeyed God's Word without Hesitation (Luke 3:3)
   A. John came as he was, maintaining simple dress and diet (Matt. 3:4; Mark 1:6).
   B. He did not demand a supernatural reassurance of his mission. Unlike the Lord Jesus, he did not see the heavens open or hear a divine voice speak at the beginning of his public ministry (Matt. 3:16, 17).
   C. "He came" indicates a voluntary coming, he was not under compulsion.
   D. He came to the whole countryside of Jordan. He did not have to go far away to be the missionary God wanted him to be.
   E. He did not equivocate about the need of the people or how their need could be met. They needed to repent and he told them so. They needed to have their sins forgiven. The baptism he was preaching demanded repentance, a change of mind (*metánoia*) before forgiveness (*áphesis*, deliverance from sin) could be obtained.

Covetousness

Key Verse: Luke 12:15

I. Introduction
   A. A subject seldom spoken about or written on.
   B. It afflicts most, if not all, men; in the church as well as outside it.
   C. Since it is a thing that will damn the soul, we need to be admonished against it, always.

II. Covetousness Defined:
   A. Inordinate (unlawful) desire. Its nature manifests itself in different ways:
      1. In the eager, anxiety to get.
      2. In a reluctance to use, dispense (1 Tim. 6:10; Luke 12:15).
   B. Idolatry (Col. 3:5).
      1. The deification of our passion, lust, desire, etc.
      2. The height of desire becomes the chief end of our labors; thus, we "worship."
      3. Since covetousness is idolatry, one who covets is an idolater.

III. The Source of Covetousness
   A. An evil heart.
   B. A carnal mind.
   C. A stubborn will—selfish, possessive.

IV. The Fruits of Covetousness
   A. Jesus warns us "beware of covetousness." Why? Not only because of what it is, but because of what it does.

1. Oppression.
   a) Jacob at the hands of Laban (Gen. 31).
   b) Micah 2:2
   c) True today.
2. Disobedience.
   Saul (1 Sam. 15:9).
B. Caused David to commit adultery (2 Sam 11:1–5).
C. Causes men to lie.
   1. Gehazi (2 Kgs. 5:20).
   2. Ananias and Sapphira (Acts 5:1–11)
   3. Prompted Achan to steal (Josh. 7).
D. Robs churches of power and strength.
   1. Balaam is not the only one guilty (2 Pet. 2:15; Jude 1:11).
   2. The potential of every congregation is greatly lessened because of this sin.
E. Leads to a departure from the faith (1 Tim. 6:10).

Leprosy Symbolizes Sin

Key Verse: Luke 17:11

I. **Ten Lepers Kept Company Together**
   A. No healthy people were among them.
   B. Their common misery drove them to each other.
   C. Their common ailment not only kept them together, but kept them at a distance from Jesus. Sin does exactly the same; it keeps people together and at a distance from Jesus.

II. **The Lepers and Jesus Came from Different Directions**
   A. The verb translated in Greek is *upéntēsen*, the past tense of *apantáō*, to encounter, to meet coming from different directions (cf. Matt. 28:9; Mark 5:2; 14:13; *apántēsis*, encounter, meeting in 1 Thess. 4:17).
   B. As far as the lepers were concerned, they were on their normal path of life. They did what they were doing daily.
   C. It was Jesus' divine providence that caused Him to be found on their pathway. Our routine is countered by His providence.

III. **Leprosy Represents Sin Which May Be Cleansed**
   A. Leprosy is a disease and all disease is the result of sin.
   B. The words for healing diseases as used in Scripture are: *therapeúō*, to heal with a demonstration of personal concern; *iáomai*, to heal or make whole without necessarily demonstrating personal concern; *sṓzō*, to save, to heal, to bring to a state or position of safety.
   C. The verb used for healing leprosy is always *katharízō*, to cleanse (cf. Matt. 8:2, 3; Mark 1:42; Luke 4:27; 17:14, 17).

D. When our Lord commissioned the Twelve, He singled out the lepers for cleansing. He said "heal the sick" (*therapeúete*): (Matt. 10:8). But is not leprosy a sickness? Jesus makes it stand separately: "cleanse the lepers" (*katharízete*).

E. When Jesus sent John the Baptist's disciples to him in prison to announce what He was doing, He commanded them to say to him, "Go and show John again those things which ye do hear and see: The blind receive their sight, and the lame walk, the lepers are cleansed, and the deaf hear, the dead are raised up, and the poor have the gospel preached to them" (Matt. 11:4, 5 [cf. Luke 7:22]).

F. Healing from the disease of leprosy is only the first part of dealing with a leprosy victim. The second part, equally as important, is the acceptance of a healed leper into the society of the healthy, and thus acceptable to worship God in the company of the others. This is the reason why healed lepers were to come to the priest to be declared cleansed (Lev. 14:1–32).

IV. **Cleansed Sinners Should Be United**
"... **the blood of Jesus Christ his Son cleanseth us from all sin**" (1 John 1:7).

A. The cleansing from sin ought to unite believers even more than their common previous misery. But while the ten lepers were together before they were cleansed, after they were cleansed they became two parties, one and nine. The Lord asserted they were all cleansed (Luke 17:17).

B. One of the desired effects of cleansing from sin is fellowship one with another: "... we have fellowship one with another ..." (1 John 1:7).

C. The difficulty of "walking in the light" is that we can so easily see the faults of our fellow cleansed lepers and

Leprosy Symbolizes Sin

separate ourselves from them. We all are clean and we can all see God (Matt. 5:8), but we do not all appreciate each other as we should. This is the tragedy of the cleansed believers.

How to Be Fully Satisfied Here and Now

Key Verses: Luke 14:16-24

I. **Wrong Concept of Christianity Being a Life of Constant Sorrow**
   A. This is a misunderstanding of the second beatitude, "Blessed are they that mourn" (Matt. 5:4).
      1. This sorrow is not due to Christ, for He came to impart joy (Luke 2:10; John 15:11).
      2. Our sorrow is the product of sin: "I will greatly multiply thy sorrow" (Gen. 3:16).
      3. Sorrow was God's foreordained consequence of man's choice to disobey Him.
   B. It is necessary for man to mourn before he can rejoice.
      1. Blessed is the person who mourns over his sin.
      2. When one recognizes what sin has done to the world and to oneself, one cannot help but mourn.
      3. It is out of that mourning (sorrow for sin) that "blessedness" is born.
   C. Joy only comes in and through Christ.
      1. The Lord, in speaking to His disciples, called them blessed, which in Greek is *makárioi* (Matt. 5:1–11).
      2. *Makários* (singular) means to be possessed with God's nature as a result of what Christ did for man.
      3. The Lord said that we are blessed because of Him.
         a) That phrase with which the beatitudes conclude in Matthew 5:11 and Luke 6:22, "for the Son of Man's sake," applied to all the beatitudes and

constitutes an explanation of how this state of blessedness, characteristic of deity, can become ours.

    b) It is because of who Christ is and what He has done that we can become what God is, blessed.

4. Blessedness is an inner condition which is unaffected by outside circumstances beyond our control (John 16:33). Circumstances may bring temporary happiness or joy, but the indwelling of God because of Christ brings blessedness.

5. This state of blessedness, and therefore full satisfaction, is not deferred to the world to come only, but begins here and now.

    a) It is equivalent to the kingdom of God. This is why in the beatitudes, whenever the promise is "the kingdom of Heaven," it is in the present tense (see Matt. 5:3, 10; Luke 6:20) whereas all the other promises are in the future.

    b) There are future rewards for present obedience. But the state of blessedness begins here and now, not only in the future as the Greeks believed.

II. The Word Blessed, *Makários,* Gave Rise to the Parable of the Great Supper.

A. The Lord was eating dinner at a Pharisee's house (Luke 14:1).

B. One of the Pharisees made a statement, "Blessed is he that shall eat bread in the kingdom of God" (Luke 14:15).

1. The verb for "shall eat" is *phágetai,* the future indicative of *esthíō,* to eat. The future indicative in Greek usually is punctiliar. It will take place at a definitive time in the future.

2. That was exactly the concept of the Jews and the Greeks: that at some time in the future God will

make possible this state of blessedness, *makariótēs*.
3. This Pharisee said, "He who will eat bread in the kingdom of God at some time in the future will experience the joy of blessedness, the joy that comes from God."
4. The parable Jesus gave was a "No" to this Pharisee in the form of a narrative.

III. The Feast Is Ready Now
A. That is the basic lesson of the parable.
  1. It is not merely a future feast.
  2. The dinner is ready.
     a) Observe the past tense "made a great supper."
     b) He bade many to come.
     c) He sent his servant to tell the invited ones to come.
B. The kingdom here is not something physical (1 Cor. 15:50; Luke 17:20, 21), but it is the state of blessedness, God indwelling man, making his heart and inner being His throne.
C. It is like bread that must be eaten in order that man may be satisfied. It is available, but it will not do you any good unless you eat it.
D. Eat it now and you will have joy now which will extend to heaven.
E. No material possessions, fields, animals, or physical relationships can be a substitute for blessedness, which comes only because of Christ and His grace.

"Look Up"

Key Verses: Luke 21:25-36

I. **Jesus Informed Us as to What to Expect in the Future.**
   A. Bible prophecy gives us hope and direction for the future (2 Pet. 1:19).
   B. Our present world is not what God meant His first creation to be. It is cursed because of man's disobedience (Gen. 3:17; Rom. 5:12), but one day it will be liberated from the slavery of corruptibility (Rom. 8:20–23).
   C. Jesus came into the world to save us spiritually, "the firstfruits of the Spirit," which we receive immediately when believing in Christ (Rom. 8:23; Eph. 1:13). In the future, however, the redemption of the environment will also take place (Rom. 8:20, 21; Rev. 21:1) as well as that of our physical bodies (Rom. 8:23; 1 Cor. 15:52–54; Phil. 3:21).

II. **What Are the Changes We Can Expect?**
   A. Despite our efforts to preach the gospel and be the salt and the light of the world (Matt. 5:13–16), things are going to get worse (2 Tim. 3:1–5).
   B. Then Christ will return, and all the believers, both dead and alive, will suddenly be caught up with Him in the air (1 Thess. 4:13–18). The Greek verb is *harpagēsómetha*, the future indicative passive, which indicates a punctiliar action of God. He will do it one time in history. It may take place at any time, which is the constant hope of the believer, or the "blessed hope" (Titus 2:13).

III. What Will Follow the Rapture of the Believers?
  A. The Great Tribulation will follow the Rapture (Matt. 24:21; Dan. 12:1; 2 Thess. 1:6ff.; Rev. 7:14).
    1. This time of trouble will not be such as we experience here and now but much accentuated.
    2. It will begin at the very time of the Rapture of the believers and last for seven years, corresponding to the seventieth week of Daniel's prophecy (Dan. 9:25–27).
  B. During this period the Antichrist will appear (Dan. 7:7, 8, 21, 25; 2 Thess. 2:3, 4; Rev. 13:11). Paul uses the term "man of sin" (2 Thess. 2:3). He is the same as the "beast" of Revelation 11:7. At first this Antichrist will protect Israel (Dan. 9:27) but then turn against it after having rebuilt the temple; and he will seek to be worshiped in lieu of the Messiah. This worship is referred to as "the abomination of desolation" (Dan. 12:11; Matt. 24:15; Mark 13:14).
  C. This period, just before the coming of Christ in glory, is that described in Luke 21:25, 26 (see also Matt. 24:29–35; Mark 13:24, 31).

IV. The Heavenly Bodies Will Be Disturbed
  A. At the end of the Great Tribulation, total destruction will occur.
    1. The sun will be darkened, and the moon will not give forth her reflected light (Matt. 24:29; Mark 13:24; Luke 21:25).
    2. The stars will fall, and the power of heaven be shaken (Matt. 24:29; Mark 13:24; Luke 21:25).
  B. Men's hearts will fail them from fear (Luke 21:26).

V. Then the Son of Man Will Come in Power and Glory (Matt. 24:30; Mark 13:26; Luke 21:27)
  A. He will finally liberate the earth from its present corruption (Rom. 8:21, 22).

"Look Up"

B. All believers will then be brought back to a new earth to live with Christ for an unprecedented millennium, to be followed by a final new heaven (Luke 21:28; Rom. 8:23; Rev. 21:1).

C. It is this glorious coming of Christ for which all believers eagerly "look up."

The Incarnation of God the Son

Key Verses: John 1:1-18

I. **The Eternal Relationship of the Father and the Son**
   A. God in His oneness is expressed by the word *Theós* without the article. In the Greek text, John 1:18 begins: "God no one ever saw. . . ." Without the article this is a reference not to a theophany, an appearance of God in a visible form, but to God in His essence as spirit—eternal and infinite.
   B. Man, and every other created being is finite, and by virtue of his finiteness cannot see or comprehend God in His infinity as spiritually self-existent. "God is spirit" (John 4:24).
   C. Whenever any man saw God or spoke with Him as Moses did (Ex. 33:11; Num. 12:8) or Adam and Eve (Gen. 2:16–25), God manifested Himself as that which could be seen and comprehended by the observer. However, He did not cease to be God, unlimited and eternal.
   D. In the eternal, infinite, and spiritual self-existence of God in John 1:1, we see God as the Logos (the Word), existing "toward the God." (The literal translation of John 1:1 is ". . . and the Word had been toward the God." The definite article is before *Theón* [*tón Theón*] referring to the Father). In John 1:18 we do not have the definite article; thus, *Theón* refers to deity in His essence as spirit, infinite and eternal.
   E. In John 1:18 we read of "the only begotten Son [*ho monogenés*, meaning not "one created" but "the only

one of the same family, the unique one"] who has always been in the bosom of the Father . . ." What is translated "which is" in Greek is *ho ōn*, the One being. This refers to His ever being in the bosom of the Father, that is, prior to His incarnation, during it, and consequent to His resurrection and ascension. These two distinct personalities of the Triune God (*theótēs*, Godhead) have never been separated even when Jesus Christ as the non-material Logos became flesh, Jesus as the God-Man on earth as He tabernacled among us (John 1:14). He never ceased to be in the bosom of the Father as God. Thus it was God the Son as Logos, Spirit, who became flesh. God became something for a time without ceasing to be what He had always been. The eternal infinite Spirit Son, the Logos, became flesh.

II. The Incarnation Was More Than a Theophany

A. It was not a mere appearance or an instantaneous manifestation for the purpose of giving a command.
B. It was becoming something He was not before. John 1:14 states "And the Word was made flesh . . ." The verb *egéneto* could more accurately be translated, "became." God cannot be made into anything, but He can become whatever He wishes. Because He was God, He could choose to become a material being. He took upon Himself that which would enable Him to live visibly and die publicly.
C. Not only did He become flesh, but He also "dwelt among us." The verb for dwelt is *eskēnōsen*, pitched a tent or temporarily tabernacled. He could have come to be here forever, but that was not His plan.

III. The Incarnation's Purpose Was Redemptive

A. He did not become flesh for His own benefit, nor to better enjoy our planet.

B. He came to redeem fallen man in fulfillment of the first prophetic announcement about redemption in Genesis 3:15.

Easy Religion

Key Verses: John 2:13-22

I. **Christ Visits the Temple During Passover**
   A. The Bible records Christ's visit to the Temple when He was twelve (Luke 2:42). Mary and Joseph came to the Passover feast every year (Luke 2:41).
   B. The Bible records Christ's visit to the temple when He was 30.
      1. Jesus came from Capernaum with "his mother and his brethren, and his disciples" (John 2:12).
      2. Joseph must have died since he is not mentioned.
   C. The Passover was a commemoration of the Exodus of the Jews from the slavery of Egypt.
   D. In New Testament times the Passover sacrifice was ritually slaughtered in the Temple.
      1. The meal could be eaten in any house within the city bounds.
      2. A company bound together by some common tie, such as Jesus and His disciples, could celebrate as though they formed a family unit.
   E. Jesus did not repudiate this Jewish tradition which was to be replaced by His death and resurrection, through which we were to be freed from sin and the dominion of the devil: "For even Christ our passover is sacrificed for us" (1 Cor. 5:7).

II. **Christ's Anger at Man's Attempt to Introduce Easy Religion**
   A. Two Greek words are rendered in English by one word, "temple."
      1. The word *hierón*, a sacred building which includes

not only the inner sanctuary, but also the courts and all the enclosures.
   2. *Naós*, is the temple or dwelling place of deity in a peculiar manner. It was the inner sanctuary. When referring to His body Jesus called it *naós*, sanctuary (John 2:21).
B. Jesus found that in the courtyard (*hierón*, John 2:14) there were "those that sold oxen and sheep and doves, and the changers of money sitting."
   1. About the sanctuary (*naós*) there were four courts: that of the priests surrounding it; that of the men toward the east; that of the women beyond; around these was an extensive court, that of the Gentiles.
   2. No one could enter the Temple without witnessing the noisy, bargaining merchants and their animals. This noise disturbed the chanting of the Levites and the prayers of the priests.
   3. The cattle and doves were a necessity for the prescribed sacrifices. The worshippers, however, ought to have brought their own sacrifices instead of waiting till the last moment to buy them. This made their religion and worship easy. They did not care about the desecration of the temple.
   4. The money changers in Greek are called *kermatistaí* (v. 14) from the verb *kermatízō* which means to divide into small money or *kérmata*, "coins."
   5. Outside the temple area they used Roman coins since the city was under Roman government. Since these Roman coins had on them the effigy of the emperor, they could not be offered for any purpose in the temple courts as this would constitute an act of desecration. So to make it easy for the worshippers, the money changers, for a percentage, changed their money.
   6. Of course, the worshippers were anxious to have little coinage to offer—"Let's get by with the least possible." Easy religion was what they were after.

Just as today many are looking for the smallest coin or a mere dollar bill to put in the offering.
7. The Lord did not approve of such desecration resulting from convenience and ease of worship. He was angry and made a whip of discarded cords and used it to chase these peddlers of easy religion out of the temple. He upturned the tables of the money changers and scattered their coins over the floor.
8. It greatly disturbs Jesus when we make His worship easy and convenient in disregard of the sacredness of His House being a House of Prayer.

Cultured But Not Born Again

Key Verses: John 3:1-17

I. Nicodemus Represents Human Wisdom
   A. He came to Jesus as a representative of the human race. "There was a man . . ." (John 3:1). The Greek word is the generic *ánthrōpos* used twice in the previous verse, "And needed not that any should testify of **man**; for he knew what was in man" (John 2:25). Because of the spiritual ignorance of men, Jesus would not entrust Himself to trust them (John 2:24).
   B. Nicodemus is a Greek name derived from the verb *nikáō*, to win, and *dḗmos*, people; a victor over the people. He lived up to his name by coming to inquire of Jesus directly, after Jesus had withdrawn Himself from the people at the Passover feast. His became the first recorded in-depth interview with Jesus. He wanted to find out about this Man for himself, despite skepticism among the other religious leaders. In his disregard for public opinion and his personal initiative in coming to Jesus directly, he is to be imitated.
   C. The fact that he was known by his Greek name indicates that Nicodemus was likely educated in the Greek culture and philosophy. Indeed, he must have been an exceptional man to be admitted into the highest court of the Jews, despite Greek connections. Nicodemus represented the upper social and religious classes of his day, as opposed to the publicans and sinners who flocked to Jesus.

D. Nicodemus may have even been a leader in politics. The Jewish historian Josephus mentions the son of a Nicodemus, Gorion, who was appointed as negotiator in the surrender of the garrison at Jerusalem in the Jewish war of 66–70 A.D. In any event, Nicodemus would have clearly been considered an outstanding man in human terms.

II. Jesus Offers Spiritual Wisdom

A. In his conversation with Jesus, however, it became immediately clear that Nicodemus was out of his element (John 3:10). He had no idea what Jesus was talking about because human wisdom does not lead to spiritual discernment (John 3:6; 1 Cor. 2:14). Nicodemus was as ignorant of his own need spiritually as were the Laodiceans (Rev. 3:17, 18).

B. Although Jesus explained spiritual reality to Nicodemus that night, it is only after Jesus' death that we see proof that he actually did become His disciple (John 19:39). Nicodemus clearly points out that the wisdom of men falls painfully short of the kingdom of God. Only by total reliance upon the work of Christ can we hope to attain it. We likewise must be "born again" (John 3:3).

What the Cross and Resurrection Can Do for You

Key Verses: John 3:14–21

I. No Salvation without the Cross
   A. The first time the Lord hinted about His death and resurrection was to the crowd at the Temple (John 2:19–22). The second time was Jesus' conversation with Nicodemus (John 3).
   B. The Lord, in describing man's need of personal salvation, refers to the incident in Numbers 21:8, 9, showing how the brazen serpent healed the serpent-bitten Israelites.
      1. There was a resemblance between the cause of the disease and the remedy. Thus Jesus identified Himself with sin, so that He might save His people from sin (2 Cor. 5:21).
      2. The serpent was lifted up so that it might be seen, and so Christ has been lifted up that He might be seen.
      3. The Israelites had their physical lives spared by looking to the serpent, but believers in Jesus receive eternal life (John 3:15).
         a) The word "eternal" signifies quality as well as duration, for being eternal, it must be the life of God.
         b) Life (*zoḗ* in Greek) characteristically (and always in John's writings) describes resurrection-life. It also denotes "course of life" (Luke 15:13; 16:25;

Rom. 6:2; Phil. 1:20), soul-life or natural vitality (John 4:50; Acts 8:33; 17:25; 1 Tim. 4:8), and life duration (James 4:14).

  c) Thus in John 3:15 "eternal life" implies the resurrection of Jesus Christ and that resurrection life which the believer receives from Christ through faith (Eph. 2:5–8).

  d) No person can be eternal except God; but as believers have God dwelling in them (1 John 4:12), they are possessed of eternal life (1 John 5:20).

 4. The brazen serpent was lifted on a pole; the Lord Jesus on the wooden cross which is often called *xúlon* "wood tree."

C. Sin ruined man, and Christ was made sin that He might save him. Christ was made sin that God might deal with him as the justice and integrity of His nature required that sin should be dealt with.

D. Evil men lifted Jesus up on the cross (John 8:28; 12:32), but God raised Him from the dead (Acts 4:10).

II. The Purpose of the Cross

A. Jesus died for a purpose, as expressed by the Greek *hína*, translated "that" in John 3:15, but meaning "for the purpose" or "so that."

B. Christ's salvation at the cross is available to all: "that whosoever" (John 3:15). The Greek word is *pás*, meaning each individual and the totality of them.

 1. This does not mean that all humanity is automatically saved because of what Jesus did on the cross.

 2. Anyone, no matter who he is (1 Cor. 12:13; Gal. 3:28), can be saved by believing. No one can claim that he or she was saved because of personal merit.

 3. Not one person could have been saved by any means other than the death and resurrection of Jesus Christ.

4. We are saved as individuals as expressed by *pás*, "anyone."

III. **The Means of Salvation**
  A. Faith that is living and constant. The verb "believeth" in Greek is a present participle, *ho pisteúōn*, "the believing one."
   1. This refers to a present state and not only to that initial exercise of faith unto salvation.
   2. To be believing, one must have had that initiation into the life of faith. Salvation has a beginning, and the life produced is continuous, not intermittent.
   3. That initial faith is expressed in Romans 10:9 where the verbs are all in the aorist subjunctive: "That if thou shalt confess with thy mouth the Lord Jesus, and shalt believe [again the aorist subjunctive, meaning that time when you are transferred from darkness to light—1 Cor. 6:11; Col. 1:13; 1 Pet. 2:9] in thine heart that God hath raised him from the dead, thou shalt be saved [in the punctiliar future passive, referring to that definitive time when you are saved by God]." If this salvation is truly of God, you are baptized into one body (1 Cor. 12:13) and become what is described in John 3:15 as *ho pisteúōn*, "the believing one."
   4. The believer cannot perish. "Should not perish:" that verb *mḗ apólētai* is in the aorist subjunctive middle which refers to anytime at which the believer can be lost. If he is a believer, at no particular time in the future will he be lost, and that is because he is *pisteúōn*, "believing." He was lost before; now he is saved and because he is saved, he will not be lost again at any time. If it were the passive voice, it would mean "He will be lost by God who saved him." The possible loss of our salvation would not

be a demonstration of our weakness, but of God's weakness. How can there be a weak God losing those whom He saved (Heb. 6:4–6)?

B. The believer has eternal life now. The verb "have" in Greek is in the subjunctive, *échē,* which means "has continuously" because at one time he was given this life which belongs exclusively to God, by God Himself because of Christ's cross and resurrection.

Jesus Before Pilate

Key Verses: John 18:33–37

I. The Jews Brought Charges Against Jesus (Luke 23:2)
   A. They said that He was perverting the nation, meaning their own Jewish nation.
   B. In addition, they accused Him of forbidding them to pay taxes to Caesar.
   C. Finally, the Jews charged that He proclaimed Himself to be a king.
   D. These charges obscured their real objection that Jesus claimed to be equal with God (John 10:33). They knew Pilate would not listen to such a religious dispute.

II. Pilate Questioned Jesus
   A. First he asked Him, "Art thou the King of the Jews?" meaning "Are you a political king ready to overthrow Roman rule?" Jesus had already refused such a kingship earlier in His ministry (John 6:15).
   B. Pilate could not imagine that there was a danger of insurrection from such a humbly-clad Galilean, who had ridden into Jerusalem on a donkey instead of in a chariot. Had Pilate believed that Jesus offered any real threat, he would never have offered Him to the Jews (John 18:31). Rather, he would have arrested Him and kept Him in prison.

III. Jesus Answered Pilate
   A. Only John records the dialogue between Jesus and Pilate (John 18:34–38).

B. By answering, Jesus acknowledged that Pilate had the authority to question him.
C. Pilate probably expected Jesus to deny that he was a king. The other evangelists tell us that Jesus answered Pilate ambiguously, "Thou sayest" (Matt. 27:11; Mark 15:2; Luke 23:3).
D. Jesus then asked Pilate if he were quoting others or really interested for His own soul (John 18:34).
E. Pilate was insulted that Jesus thought he was involved in a Jewish religious matter: "Am I a Jew?" He added that Jesus' own people had brought this charge against Him.

IV. Jesus Explained His Kingdom (John 18:36, 37)
A. First, He said what it was not: "My kingdom is not of this world." His kingdom did not originate with men but with God (John 18:36). "Kingdom," *basileía*, is better translated kingship. Had Jesus' kingship been earthly, His subjects, *hupērétai*, would have fought to preserve His rule.
B. Jesus then said what His kingdom was (John 12:37).
  1. Pilate was completely confused by Jesus' explanation because he was totally unaware of spiritual truth. That is why he burst into the direct questions: "Art thou a king then?" The interrogative *oukoún* used by Pilate is derived from the negative particle *ou* (*ouk* before a vowel) and *oún*, therefore, "not therefore." It requires a positive answer and has the force of an affirmative, not a question: "Thou art then a king?"
  2. Jesus agreed with Pilate that He was a king, but king of "the truth" (John 18:37). "What is truth?" Pilate asked, expecting no answer. He then declared to the Jews that Jesus was innocent (John 18:38).

V. **Jesus Asserted His Humanity and His Deity**
   A. "To this end was I born, . . ." was a declaration of His humanity. The verb *gegénnēmai* is the perfect indicative passive of *gennáō*, to give birth to. It should be translated, "I have been born." "To this end" refers to the purpose of Jesus' humanity — to become the perfect sacrifice for sin. The Jews and Pilate were actually acting as agents in accomplishing the goal of Christ's birth.
   B. "And for this cause came I into the world." While *gegénnēmai* is passive in meaning, the verb *elḗlutha*, I came, is the active voice of *érchomai*, I come. Jesus' deity is shown in that He came into this world from another, of His own volition in response to his Father's will (John 3:17, 34; 5:36, 38; 6:29). Being God, he is indeed King not only of earth but of heaven (Matt. 28:18).
   C. Jesus came as a witness to the truth. The verb translated "that I should bear witness" is *hína marturḗsō*, for the purpose of bearing witness once and for all. His death and resurrection were to be the final proof of His deity. "To the truth" does not refer to truth in general, but to the truth of His incarnation, crucifixion and resurrection for our salvation (1 Cor. 15:1–4).
   D. "Every one that is of the truth heareth my voice" (John 18:37). The verb "hear," *akoúō*, means to both hear and obey (Matt. 10:14; 17:5; 18:15; Mark 6:11; Luke 10:16; John 5:24). One cannot do either, however, unless he is born again (John 3:3). Pilate was not and, therefore, completely misunderstood the kingdom Jesus described.

How We Are Justified Before God

Key Verses: Romans 4:1-5

I. Man Cannot Be Justified by Doing the Works of the Law (Rom. 3:20)
   A. Being dead in our sins and trespasses before our justification, we cannot perform any good spiritual works (Eph. 2:1). For anybody to work, he must first have life. Therefore, it is impossible for a sinful person to achieve salvation through his own efforts.
      1. The Apostle Paul presents the example of Abraham in Romans 4:1: "What shall we say then that Abraham our father, as pertaining to the flesh, hath found?" The phrase "pertaining to the flesh" means regarding his external performances, his works, what he did in his life of spiritual deadness. The expression "pertaining to the flesh" stands in contrast to "being in the spirit" (Rom. 7:6).
      2. In Romans 4:2, Paul presents the supposition: "For if Abraham were justified by works, he hath whereof to glory; but not before God." If Abraham were justified by works, then he would not glorify God but himself. Such a self-induced salvation by works would tend to make a person proud. And the Scriptures clearly state that pride is a sin detestable to God (Ps. 10:2; 73:6; Prov. 11:2; 16:18; 21:4).
      3. In fact, Abraham could not be justified by the deeds of the law, because the law was not even given until many years after his death.

B. The law, given by God through Moses, actually compounded man's sinfulness by turning general sin into direct disobedience of specific laws (Rom. 7:7–9). As Paul shows, we cannot be saved by the law but only be made more aware of our own sinfulness through it.

II. **Man Can Only Be Justified by Faith in Christ (Rom. 4:3)**

A. "For what saith the Scripture?" Observe that Paul does not say "the Scriptures" but "the Scripture" in Romans 4:3, referring to a particular Old Testament Scripture, namely Genesis 15:6, "And he believed in the Lord; and he counted it to him for righteousness" (see also Gal. 3:6; James 2:23).

B. What does the expression "Abraham believed God" encompass? (Rom. 4:3)

1. Read carefully Genesis chapters 15 to 18. You will find that God made a covenant with Abraham. God said to him in Genesis 17:7, "And I will establish my covenant between me and thee and thy seed after thee in their generations, for an everlasting covenant, to be a God unto thee and to thy seed after thee." When Abraham heard about his seed, he "fell upon his face, and laughed, and said in his heart, Shall a child be born unto him that is a hundred years old? and shall Sarah, that is ninety years old, bear?" (Gen. 17:17). What the Lord was actually foretelling was that the Messiah was going to be born from Abraham's seed. In effect, God was announcing to him His plan of redemption in and through the Lord Jesus Christ. And Abraham believed God, even though his understanding was limited to his own small part in the drama.

2. Furthermore, when God asked Abraham to sacrifice Isaac (Gen. 22), He was providing a symbol of

the future sacrifice that was going to take place when the seed of Abraham, Jesus Christ, came into the world. How aptly our Lord Jesus answered the Jews who were priding themselves for being the descendants of Abraham when He said to them in John 8:56, "Your father Abraham rejoiced to see my day: and he saw it and was glad." Symbolically, Abraham was shown how he and all the rest of God's people were going to be saved. Whereas Abraham dimly saw this salvation in the future, we can clearly see Christ's atonement in the past.
- C. "And it was counted unto him for righteousness" (Rom. 4:3). God justified Abraham as he showed his faith in God in such situations as being willing to sacrifice his own son in obedience to God's command. Because of this observable faith, God took Abraham's guilt and placed it upon the Lord Jesus Christ, whose righteousness was then imputed to Abraham.
- D. One of the most important verbs in this Scripture is what is translated variably as "was counted" (v. 3); "reckoned" (v. 4); "counted" (v. 5); "imputeth" (vv. 6, 8). This verb means to put it down in the books and then to take for granted that what was once owed to God, is owed no longer. In the meantime, someone else has paid it.

III. **Thus Concerning the Process of Justification, We May Infer the Following Truths:**
- A. Negatively, there is no work of the flesh that we may do as Gentiles or Jews to placate God's justice since the sin of Adam.
- B. The only sacrifice that could satisfy God's justice is a perfect sacrifice, which could only be found in the sinless Son of God who came into the world to give His life as a ransom for us.

C. When man accepts and considers this sacrifice of Jesus Christ as replacement for the punishment of his own sin, then it is imputed unto him as righteousness. On the contrary, if one does not recognize himself as ungodly and worthless; then it is impossible for him to be justified by God. The realization of one's own helplessness and sinfulness is the first step toward salvation.

D. Faith in Christ and His substitutionary work for us causes God to declare us not guilty any more. This is a judicial act (Rom. 4:6–8; 5:18, 19; 8:33, 34; 2 Cor. 5:19–21). It is then that God considers His law fulfilled in Christ on behalf of the sinner (Rom. 3:26; 8:3; 2 Cor. 5:21; Gal. 3:13; 1 Pet. 3:18). Besides the objective side of justification, there is also the subjective aspect whereby the believer is assured of his complete forgiveness of all sins (Rom. 5:1, 11, 15, 17–19, 21; 1 John 1:9; Ps. 103:12). Furthermore, there is a restoration of the fallen creature into a forgiven sinner who now finds favor with God through the imputation of Christ's righteousness (Rom. 5:11; 1 Cor. 1:30).

E. Justification is entirely an act of God and leads to sanctification. We are sanctified in Him, both as a work that He has accomplished (Phil. 1:6; Heb. 10:14) and also as a cooperative new creature that seeks to please God (Gal. 2:20).

What Is Justification?

Key Verses: Romans 5:1-5

I. Introduction
   A. The subject of the entire Epistle to the Romans is man's justification before God through Christ.
   B. The verb "to justify" (*dikaiō* in Greek) is a legal term meaning to acquit, to declare righteous; the opposite of condemn (Rom. 8:33).
   C. Synonyms of "justify" are "reckon righteous" (Rom. 4:5, 6), "remit sins" (Rom. 4:7), "not reckon sin" (Rom. 4:8).
   D. Only the judge can justify the accused or offer pardon. Ordinary man cannot do it.
   E. The verb "justify" occurs 39 times in the New Testament and 29 of these usages are by Paul.
   F. The result of this justifying is called justification (*dikaíōsis*).
   G. This justification God does not declare unless two things are accomplished:
      1. The person is truly born again by the power and energy of the Holy Spirit (John 3:3–8).
         a) This does not involve a mere decision by man, but it is God's acceptance of man's decision as genuine. At that time, man as a believer is attached to the body of Christ (1 Cor. 12:13).
         b) Christ indwells the believer and lives in him (Phil. 1:21).
         c) The old Adamic nature still exists warring against Christ within (Rom. 7:23).
      2. There is a working out of Christ's salvation. Justification involves a new creature (2 Cor. 5:17) and

not the creation of a corpse, which is what James calls "dead faith," that is, good for nothing (James 2:14–26). That salvation which Christ gives is the believer's very own and he is responsible to work it out to manifest it in daily living. If one does not, He does not have His life within you, but is simply under a delusion that he is saved.

II. **Justification Is a Once-and-for-All Accomplishment by Christ**
   A. Romans 5:1 begins with the verb *dikaiōthéntes*, which is an aorist passive participle. It should be translated, "Since we were justified." This means:
      1. That someone other than ourselves did it and that is Christ: "through our Lord Jesus Christ" (v. 1).
         a) This excludes the law which was given to identify and punish sin, but not to remove it and forgive it (Rom. 2:12; 3:20, 21, 27, 28, 31; 4:15; 5:13; 8:3; Gal. 2:16, 21; 3:11, 12, 21, 23; 4:5). This law was a schoolmaster leading us to Christ (Rom. 10:4; Gal. 3:24).
         b) The law is not only that which God delivered to Moses, both moral and ceremonial, but also our own conscience, the innate law of God within us (Rom. 2:15).
      2. Jesus Christ took the initiative to become flesh (John 1:1, 4) and to die for us. God knew Adam and Eve would misuse the freedom of choice He gave them, and therefore He made provision in Jesus Christ becoming the Lamb of God before the foundation of the world (Heb. 9:26; 1 Pet. 3:19–21; Rev. 13:8; 17:8). Even His choice of us was before the foundation of the world (Eph. 1:4).
         a) Through His death He justified us before the Father.
         b) This means that the Father God accepted His Son's sacrifice on our behalf as a once-and-for-all

atonement for our sins. Before its actual accomplishment, it was forever accepted in the planning of it in the eternal councils of the Godhead. This is why everyone ever saved before Christ actualized His sacrifice, and ever since is saved by this sacrifice alone (Acts 4:12). Even Abraham was saved through faith in the Christ, who as the Word (John 1:1–5) preceded Abraham (John 8:58). Abraham rejoiced in seeing by faith Christ's day of atonement (John 8:56; Rom. 4:1–3, 9, 16; Gal. 3:6, 8).

B. Justification is an accomplished fact. In the Councils of the Godhead it was planned and it was effective before it was actualized. It is the only basis on which God declares us justified, removes our guilt of original and personal sin and regenerates us, making us righteous (2 Cor. 5:21). The basic word from which justification is derived is *díkē*, which means justice or right. When we are justified by God through Christ, then not only do we know what God expects of us as His rights, but we are given the power to render unto Him what is His. We are clothed with His righteousness (Rom. 6:18, 19; 10:4; 1 Cor. 1:30; 2 Cor. 5:21; Eph. 6:14; Phil. 1:11; 3:9).

III. How Does Christ's Justification of the Sinner Become a Reality in Man?

A. "Through faith" (Rom. 5:1). Faith means accepting that which Christ did for us as a substitute for what we could not do for our own salvation.

1. This faith appropriates what is available as our very own.
2. It is not by heredity, but something each one must do himself (Rom. 1:16; 3:22; 4:5, 24; 9:33; 10:4, 9–11; Eph. 1:13, 19). "Believe on the Lord Jesus Christ, and thou shalt be saved, and thy house" (Acts 16:31).

B. This faith is not some quality that is abstract. It is only as good as the person on whom it is based. Romans 5:1 says, "Therefore being justified by faith . . . through our Lord Jesus Christ." Faith in anyone else will not declare a person not guilty of sin and give him the power against sin. It has to be on the One who bore our sin on His own body and that body was the one in whom the fullness of the Godhead dwelt (Rom. 8:3; 1 Cor. 15:3; 2 Cor. 5:21; Gal. 1:4; Heb. 9:28; 1 Pet. 2:24; 3:18; 4:1; 1 John 1:7, 9; 2:29; 4:10; Rev. 1:5).

The Results of Our Justification

Key Verses: Romans 5:1-11

I. Justification Is a Historical Event
   A. Two men, Adam and Jesus, have profoundly affected man's relationship to God and, in turn, have affected the whole course of history.
      1. In Romans 5:6, Paul states that Christ died for the ungodly. The Greek word for "ungodly" is *asebeís*, meaning those without any reverence toward God. The first man and woman, Adam and Eve, proved indifferent to God. They did not believe Him when He told them what would happen to them if they disobeyed Him (Gen. 2:17; 3:3). As a result of their unbelief, all humans fell from God's favor, "for all have sinned, and come short of the glory of God" (Rom. 3:23). To "come short of the glory of God" means to be incapable of recognizing God for all that He is and to fall short of being what He intended man to be. The fall of man was due to the sin of his representative, Adam. Adam's disobedience was a definite historical event which had lasting consequences for the human race.
      2. The countermeasure of Adam's sin and man's fall was Jesus Christ's sacrifice and our resulting justification (Rom. 4:25). Jesus was delivered up for our offenses by God, His Father, who had foreordained it before the foundation of the world (Gen. 3:15; Rev. 13:8). Jesus was then raised by the Father, the One who delivered Him (Acts 13:30; Rom. 10:9;

1 Cor. 6:14). Also the Holy Spirit is said to have raised Jesus from the dead (Rom. 8:11). But Jesus raised Himself from the dead. In 1 Corinthians 15:4 it is the perfect passive, *egḗgertai*, with middle meaning that is used, and which should be translated "He has raised himself." The same tense is also used in 1 Corinthians 15:12, 13, 20. His resurrection was by His own volition and strength, proving that He was equal with God, the Father and the Holy Spirit. The birth, death, and resurrection of Jesus Christ are all irrefutable historical realities. He was the last Adam who came into the world to cancel out the destruction caused by the first Adam's sin.

B. There is a difference, however, between the way sin passed on to all humanity and the way the gift of grace provided by Christ's death operates in the lives of human beings.
   1. This is made clear in Romans 5:15, "But not as the offense [transgression, specific disobedience of Adam, *paráptōma*], so also is the free gift [*chárisma*, the result of grace or *cháris*]." What is the difference then between the offense that we inherited from Adam and the free gift of salvation made available for us?
   2. The sin of Adam passed on automatically to all by bequeathing to us a sinful nature. This is why we die. When we sin, we sin not simply because Adam sinned, but also because we choose to continue in sin. For our own sin we squarely bear the responsibility. None of us would perish simply because Adam sinned, but because we chose to sin.
   3. The gift of grace won by Christ does not pass automatically to all, but must be appropriated by us as individuals through faith in Christ (John 1:12). We are condemned not because we are merely

human, but because we choose not to believe on the Lord Jesus (John 3:18). But even when we believe, we cannot escape the consequence of Adam's sin which is physical death. Faith in Christ liberates us from spiritual death which is spiritual separation from God.

II. **For Christ's Sacrifice to Become Effective in Our Individual Lives, We Must Believe That His Death Atoned for Adam's and Our Own Sins**
   A. Paul clearly states this fact in Romans 5:1: "Therefore being justified by faith, we have peace with God through our Lord Jesus Christ." The verb is in the aorist passive participle, *dikaiōthéntes*, "Because we were justified."
      1. Our justification was accomplished by Jesus Christ, "... through our Lord Jesus Christ." He did it all; once and for all.
      2. Faith in Christ makes the justification Christ earned my very own. It affects my life. It declares me not guilty before God and washes away my sin (Is. 1:18).
      3. No more do I have disturbing guilt in my heart, mind and conscience. I am not afraid that at any moment I may be called before my maker and condemned. To the contrary, I have "peace with God." In Greek it is "We have peace toward God." The definite article indicates "the God" as "the Father" whom I have offended.
      4. I am not the only one who has this peace. Note, Paul does not say "I have peace," but "we have peace." The moment I am reconciled to God I become a member of the brotherhood of believers who also have this peace.
   B. This "peace with God" is for both the here and now and for eternity. As Paul expresses it in Philippians 1:21, both life and death are gain to the believer.

The Results of Our Justification

III. Through Our Faith in Christ We Have Access to God
   A. "By whom also we have access by faith unto this grace . . ." (Rom. 5:2). The Greek is *diá*, through, whom, that is, Jesus Christ. The word "access" is *prosagōgḗ*, a leading to (also in Eph. 2:18; 3:12). Having access to God might be likened to being introduced into the presence of a potentate, who besides being a father, still is a king. Every time we approach our heavenly Father we must be conscious of the fact that Jesus Christ stands by us listening to our every conversation. He taught us to always pray "in His name" (John 14:13, 14; 15:16; 16:23, 24). We must never abuse this access and must guard against indiscreet familiarity with God or commanding Him to do our will.
   B. The verb translated "we have" is *eschḗkamen*, the perfect indicative of *échō*. It indicates that there was a time when knowing God became a reality in our lives, continues now, and will continue in the future.
   C. Our access is "by faith." Faith means believing that we shall be granted that which the sovereign God deems appropriate for us to have. As a loving Father, He will not let us have everything we want, but rather in His infinite wisdom, He discerns what we need. God's purpose is always our closer relationship with Himself.
   D. Prayer or access to God is always "a grace." "By whom also we have access by faith into this grace wherein we stand." The word is *cháris*, which means favor that we do not deserve. This grace has the power to transform our prayers to God so that we conform to His will instead of demanding our own way (Rom. 8:26).

IV. We Also Stand in Christ Because of Our Faith and Have Hope
   A. The verb used is *estḗkamen*, the perfect indicative of *hístēmi*, to stand. That means that there was a time

when we were dead in our sins (Eph. 2:1), and because we believed in Christ, we began to stand, we were resurrected with Him (Eph. 2:6; Col. 2:12; 3:1) and we shall continue to stand.

B. "And rejoice in hope of the glory of God." We are not supposed to boast in anything of ourselves, but when we appropriate Christ's justification, we have much to celebrate. The word "rejoice" is actually "boast," *kauchōmetha*.

C. Our boast is in the grace of God experienced here and now, but particularly in the hope of what is yet to be.

D. In eternity we shall have the privilege of knowing God as He is because we shall be like Him (1 John 3:2).

The Believer's Conflict With Sin

Key Verses: Romans 7:14-25

I. **When We Believe on the Lord Jesus, He Enters Our Hearts and Lives in Us**
   A. Through faith we are declared righteous by God (Rom. 5:1) and accepted as His children (John 1:12).
   B. Through faith we are cleansed by the blood of Christ (Rom. 5:9; 1 John 1:9) and changed in our inner selves as well as in our outward standing with God. As such, we are transferred from the kingdom of darkness into the kingdom of light (Acts 26:18; Col. 1:13; 1 Thess. 5:4, 5; 1 Pet. 2:9; 1 John 1:6). This reconciliation *katallagē* (Rom. 5:11), transforms our former enmity with God, into friendship (Rom. 5:10).

II. **But the Believer Continues to Live in the Same Human Body and Struggles with Sin**
   A. We are mortal (*thnētoí*), and therefore, subject to physical decay and death. Because we are in the body, we are called *sárkinoi* (Rom. 7:14, "fleshy, corpulent, made of flesh"). This present composition of our earthly personality we cannot help. Christ is also in our mortal body, however (Rom. 8:11; 2 Cor. 4:11), and the time will one day come when our flesh will be redeemed (Rom. 8:23; 1 Cor. 15:53, 54).
   B. We may either let our bodies control our spirits or vice-versa. In 1 Corinthians 3:1, Paul calls the Corinthian believers *sarkikoí*, "carnal," as contrasted to mature, spirit-controlled believers. A carnal Christian

is one who allows his natural body to pull him down rather than permitting his redeemed spirit to lift him up. This state is to be distinguished from that of the unbeliever, who has a mind-set after the flesh (Rom. 8:5–9, 12, 13). Through faith the believer is crucified with Christ and his flesh no longer has preeminence in his life (Rom. 6:6; Gal. 2:20). The dedicated believer continues to put down his old nature, which is a continuous struggle for the rest of his life. It is this battle which Paul describes in Romans 7:14–25.

C. Furthermore, we as believers must also contend with an unredeemed environment (Rom. 8:20–22).

III. The Believer Does Not Continually Sin Willfully

A. "For that which I do, I allow not: for what I would, that do I not; but what I hate, that do I" (Rom. 7:15). A believer cannot love the evil that he does. What he hates, he will cease to do. Conversely, he cannot have the mind-set (*phrónēma*) of the flesh and be willfully obedient to the Spirit of God (Rom. 8:7).

B. "Now then it is no more I that do it, but sin that dwelleth in me: (Rom. 7:17). This "I" refers to the new man that the believer receives in Christ Jesus along with the indwelling of the Holy Spirit and this new spiritual creation desires no sin and does no sin, but is the renewed image of God. This contrasts with and is in conflict with the fleshly part of the believer who is pulled toward sin and continues in sin (Rom. 7:18–21).

IV. Victory, However, Is Possible at All Times

A. The battle described in Romans 7 closes on a triumphant note: "I thank God through Jesus Christ our Lord. So then with the mind I myself serve the law of God [I do what God expects of me]; but with the flesh the law of sin" (Rom. 7:25). I do not serve the law of sin; only the unredeemed flesh in which I dwell serves the law of sin.

B. The final victory of the Christian life is then described in Romans 8:37, "Nay, in all these things we are more than conquerors through him that loved us." This is the only place in the New Testament where the verb *hupernikáō*, "to be more than conqueror," occurs. Through the power of the indwelling Spirit we can defeat that subtle enemy of our souls.

Who Cannot Please God?

Key Verse: Romans 8:8

I. The Inevitability of the Flesh
   A. Flesh indicates the literal, material body which houses the spiritual part of man. This is his soul (*psuchḗ*), which enables him to communicate with his environment and his spirit (*pneúma*), which enables him to communicate with God. This cannot be the meaning in Romans 8:8 where Paul says, ". . . they that are in the flesh cannot please God." All human beings, believers and unbelievers alike, are "in the flesh" or in the body (cf. Rom. 8:3, where flesh refers to the incarnation of Jesus Christ.)
   B. Flesh also means the earthly sphere of existence (John 1:14). This cannot be the meaning of Romans 8:8. Jesus came to save human beings on earth.
   C. Those who are "in the flesh" means those who are ruled by their bodily appetites and desires.
   D. Thus far in Romans 8 Paul has used the word *sárx*, flesh, nine times, as the opposite of the *pneúma*, spirit. He emphasized the fact that the unregenerate person not only walks according to the flesh (v. 1, 4) but is according to the flesh (v. 5). This cannot be true of the believer who walks according to the Spirit (v. 5; Gal. 5:16).
   E. The believer before his new birth is said to have been in the flesh. "For when we were in the flesh the motions [*pathḗmata*, passions] of sins, which were by the law, did work in our members to bring forth fruit unto death" (Rom. 7:5). The phrase here is *en*, in, *tḗ sarkí*,

the flesh. It is with the same preposition as the word *sárx* is used in Romans 8:8, while up to now it has been according to the flesh (vv. 1, 4, 5). The unbeliever is presented as walking according to the flesh (vv. 1, 4), and as being according to the flesh (v. 5). Sinful nature is the guide of an unbeliever. In verse 8 however, the preposition changes to *en*, in. The unbelievers who cannot please God are "in the flesh." They are totally immersed in their sinful nature (cf. Rom. 7:18).

II. What Is the Lifestyle of Those in the Flesh?
A. It is habitually doing the works of the flesh, which are listed in Galatians 5:19–21. They are:
1. Adultery (*moicheía*). A person cannot be a married person and live with extramarital relationships and be pleasing to God.
2. Fornication (*porneía*) which is sexual immorality of any kind, that is, homosexuality, lesbianism, or any other kind than that which God instituted as belonging in a legitimate, monogamous, marital relationship.
3. Uncleanness (*akatharsía*) is moral lewdness as opposed to chastity (cf. Rom. 1:24; 1 Thess. 4:7; Eph. 4:19; 2 Cor. 6:17).
4. Lasciviousness (*asélgeia*), which is excess, not in moderation.
5. Idolatry (*eidōlolatreía*) which is partaking of things offered to idols (cf. 1 Cor. 10:14) or of the vices usually connected with sacrifices to idols. It also means making an idol, equating anybody or anything with God and worshipping it.
6. Witchcraft, which includes drug consumption, resulting in trances.
7. Hatred (*échthrai*, the plural of *échthra*) or enmities (cf. James 4:4; Eph. 2:15, 16).

8. Variance (*éreis*, the plural of *éris*, strife, contention) (cf. Rom. 1:29; 13:13; 1 Cor. 1:11; 3:3; 2 Cor. 12:20; Phil. 1:15; 1 Tim. 6:4; Titus 3:9). This refers to fights resulting from rivalry.
9. Emulations (*zéloi*, the plural of *zélos*, jealousy or jealousies cf. Acts 13:45; Rom. 13:13; 1 Cor. 3:3; 2 Cor. 12:20; James 3:14, 16).
10. Wrath (*thumoí*, the plural of *thumós*, anger), outbursts of anger, bad temper, rage.
11. Strife (*eritheíai*, the plural of *eritheía*, party strife, contention, rivalry); (cf. Rom. 2:8; 2 Cor. 12:20; Phil. 1:17; 2:3; James 3:14, 16).
12. Seditions (*dichostasíai*, the plural of *dichostasía*, dissension) bringing divisions among people.
13. Heresies (*hairéseis*, the plural of *haíresis*, discord, dissension, cf. 1 Cor. 11:19; 2 Pet. 2:1). These are self-willed opinions against the truth.
14. Envyings (*phthónoi*, the plural of *phthónos*, envy). These are feelings of displeasure which one experiences when hearing of the success or advantage of others (cf. Matt. 27:18; Mark 15:10; Rom. 1:29; Phil. 1:15; 1 Tim. 6:4; Titus 3:3; 1 Pet. 2:1; James 4:5).
15. Murders (*phónoi*, the plural of *phónos*, murder), the killing of men (cf. Matt. 15:19; Mark 7:21; Rev. 9:21).
16. Drunkenness (*méthai*, the plural of *méthē*), drunken (cf. Luke 21:34; Rom. 13:13; Gal. 5:21).
17. Revelings (*kómoi*, the plural of *kómos*, a carousing or merry-making. There was a custom in New Testament times of going, after supper, into the streets and through the city with torches, music and songs in honor of Bacchus, the god of wine.) (See Rom. 13:13; 1 Pet. 4:3.)

B. Those who lead a lifestyle in the flesh shall not inherit the kingdom of God (Gal. 5:21).

III. Such People Cannot Please God
  A. In verse 7 Paul told us that the mind-set of the flesh does not and cannot subject itself to the law of God.
  B. In verse 8 he tells us that individuals with such a mind-set cannot please God, even if they perform any particular act that in itself might be pleasing to God. This is indicated by the use of the aorist infinitive *arésai*, to please, involving a particular act. Individual acts of goodness cannot make up for a life of rebellion against God.

IV. What Does "Pleasing God" Mean?
  A. The Greek word is *arésai*, the aorist infinitive of *arésko*, to please. Originally *arésko* meant "to set up a positive relation." People with a mind-set and lifestyle of the flesh have no positive relationship with God.
  B. The only way to please God is to be born again by the Spirit of God and live a life of holiness or a life in the Spirit.
  C. How we walk is what pleases God. Paul's advice to the Thessalonians (1 Thess. 4:1) is what we as believer need to heed: "how (we) ought to walk and to please God." The verbs *peripateín*, walk, and *aréskein* are both in the present infinitive, which means constant walking and pleasing and not an occasional act to please God, as the unbelievers try to do, though they cannot achieve their end.

How You Can Be Saved

Key Verses: Romans 10:8-13

I. Every Person Has the Opportunity to Be Saved
   A. "That if thou shalt . . ." in Romans 10:9 is given without qualification and applies to everyone, "Jew and the Greek" (v. 12) "for whosoever shall call upon the name of the Lord shall be saved" (v. 13).
   B. Salvation is specifically offered to individuals, "If thou shalt confess . . ." and not to groups.

II. Confession Is Agreeing with God That We Are Sinful
   A. It is the Holy Spirit who brings conviction to the heart of man (John 16:8; Eph. 2:8).
   B. The verb "confess" is *homológēsēs* derived from *homoú*, together, and *légō*, to say. Thus, a person first believes together with God that he is a sinner and then externalizes this agreement with his mouth (v. 10).
   C. Why "with thy mouth" (v. 9)? In this way we verify our faith and its personal application—unlike a certain young lady who when asked whether she was saved said, "My mother told me I was when I was a little girl."

III. There Is an Initial Confession and Continuous Confessions
   A. The verb *homológēsēs* is in the aorist subjunctive which describes an initial confession. This initial confession indicates a change in our position from darkness to light, from death to life, or a rebirth (John 3:3).
   B. Consequent to that transforming experience, one must continue to confess his sins to God for forgiveness (1 John 1:9).

C. The verb "believe" is also in the aorist subjunctive, meaning that our faith and confession of it is an accomplished fact, which makes us continuing believers.

IV. **What Must We Believe to Be Saved?**
A. We must confess that God raised Jesus from the dead (v. 9). Without faith in the resurrection there can be no salvation (1 Cor. 15:14). *Ho Theós* (the God) here refers to the Father (see John 1:1; Eph. 1:17; Gal. 1:4).
B. But since Jesus is Lord, He also raised Himself (Rom. 6:9). Here *egertheís*, raised, is in the middle tense and should be translated, having raised Himself. The same tense for "raised" is used in Romans 8:34 and also in John 2:19; 10:17 and 1 Corinthians 15:20.
C. The Holy Spirit, being part of the Triune God, also raised Jesus from the dead (Rom. 8:11).

V. **The Result of This Belief and Confession Is Salvation**
A. The verb used for "thou shalt be saved," is *sōthēsē*. It is in the aorist subjunctive passive voice, which indicates a definite and final result.
B. The passive tense means our salvation is an act of God, not of ourselves, and, thus can never be taken away. As Jesus promised, "And I give unto them eternal life; and they shall never perish, neither shall any man pluck them out of my hand" (John 10:28).

Man's Responsibility Toward God

Key Verses: Romans 12:1-13

I. God's Sovereignty Does Not Absolve Man of His Personal Responsibility
   A. One truth clearly taught in Scripture is that God is sovereign in His thoughts, plans, and executions. This was elaborated by Paul in Romans 9—11, especially as he deals with God's relationship with Israel and the Gentiles. In His sovereignty it is impossible for God to be unjust toward anyone.
   B. A second related and parallel truth is that man is responsible for all that God has given him, as shown in the Parable of the Pounds (Luke 19:11–27) and the Parable of the Talents (Matt. 25:14–30). It is true that God by His grace affects a work of regeneration in us (1 Pet. 1:3; Rom. 5:10; 2 Cor. 5:18). But as a new creature in Christ, a believer becomes personally responsible for his actions and the impression that he makes on the world around him. In other words, the believer must make his own decisions and be held accountable for them. In Romans 12, Paul stresses that the believer's main responsibility is to live a holy life.

II. We Must Consecrate Our Bodies to Christ
   A. When we become Christians, we must recognize that we do not automatically get rid of our corruptible, mortal bodies (Rom. 6:12; 1 Cor. 15:53, 54; 2 Cor. 4:11; 5:4); this transformation will not occur until the final resurrection (Rom. 8:23).

B. It is the indwelling Spirit of the crucified and resurrected Christ (Rom. 6:6; Gal. 2:20) who gives us the power to voluntarily refrain from sin (Rom. 6:14). And, thus, only as a Christian am I in a position to present my body unto the Lord instead of unto sin.
1. This act of consecration discussed in Romans 12:1 takes two forms. The verb *parastḗsai* is in the infinitive aorist which indicates one act of surrender of the body. A daily, moment by moment denial of our body to be used for unrighteousness can only be achieved by this once-and-for-all presentation of ourselves unto God as being alive from the dead. In the phrase "now yield your members servants to righteousness . . ." (Rom. 6:19), the verb is the aorist imperative of *parístēmi*, "to present," indicating a once-and-for-all presentation or voluntary crucifixion with Christ (Gal. 2:20).
2. The second form this consecration of our bodies takes after our initial dedication to Christ is called "a living sacrifice" (Rom. 12:1). The participial adjective *zōsan*, "living" means something that is the result of our present will and which is done constantly without ever becoming dead or losing its vibrancy. A "sacrifice" is something that we give up in order to please God. Such a sacrifice does not mean the privation of the legitimate needs of our body within the realm of prescribed Christian conduct. This unselfish yielding must not only be living, conscious and constant, but also holy, separated from sin and attached to God. It must also be well-pleasing or acceptable unto God and it must have a calculated or reasoned-out purpose and public usefulness. That is what *latreía*, "service," is. Our sacrifice must also be *logikḗ*, "reasonable, logical, well-planned and calculated." God will not accept as service that which has

selfish motives and neglects our duty toward our family and society.

III. We Must Be Non-Conformists

A. "And be not conformed to this world or age . . ." (Rom. 12:2). We must remain apart from the world because this age does not have the mind of Christ. The verb in Greek is *suschēmatízesthe*, from *sún*, "together," and *schḗma*, "the outward shape or fashion." We should not dress or behave as the people of our age if they do not conform to God's standard. The verb is in the present imperative indicating that we should constantly refuse to conform to the age.

B. ". . . but ye be transformed by the renewing of your mind . . ." (Rom. 12:2). The verb Paul uses is *metamorphoústhe*, from *metá*, denoting change of condition, and *morphóō*, "to form." The noun *morphḗ* refers to the inner disposition of the heart versus the *schḗma* in the previous verb, which means "the outward fashion." When we bring about an inner change of mind, there will be a difference in the way we behave outwardly.

The Prudent Use of Our Liberty in Christ

Key Verses: Romans 14:1-23

I. When Christ Saves Us, He Frees Us from the Bondage of Sin
   A. An unredeemed man is a slave to sin (Rom. 6:17, 20). Every time he exercises his choice, it is to sin because he is a sinner by nature (Eph. 2:2, 3).
   B. Such a person is under the delusion that he is free, but in reality he is among "the servants of corruption" (2 Pet. 2:19).
   C. The redeemed person, on the other hand, does not automatically and habitually choose to sin. "Whosoever abideth in him [Christ] sinneth not [*hamartánei*, 'continually and naturally']: whosoever sinneth [*ho hamartánōn*, 'continuously and naturally'] hath not seen him, neither known him" (1 John 3:6).
   D. Nevertheless, the Christian may fall into sin occasionally. Such occurrences, however, are not God's will for us. "These things I write unto you, that ye sin not" (*hamártēte*, the aorist subjunctive, meaning "that ye may not sin at anytime"). John continues to explain, "and if any man sin [*hamártē*, aorist subjunctive, meaning "fall into a single act of sin"], we have an advocate with the Father, Jesus Christ the righteous" (1 John 2:1). It is because the Christian may be influenced by his old nature, the sinful environment in which he lives, or his deficient study and understanding of God's Word, that God has made provision for such an occasional lapse into sin.

The Prudent Use of Our Liberty in Christ

II. **Christianity Is a Religion of Volitional Slavery**
   A. The redeemed person becomes a voluntary slave to Jesus Christ (Rom. 1:1; Phil. 1:1; Jude 1:1).
   B. At the same time, he is still free to choose good or evil, realizing that there are God-ordained consequences which necessarily follow each decision.
   C. In the New Testament culture, to be freed from slavery was called *huiós, huiothesía*, "adoption, becoming a son" (Gal. 4:5–7). A Christian in like manner becomes a willing slave to Christ instead of an unwilling one to sin. If he does happen to sin, this act does not alter his new status as a child of God.

III. **Romans 14 Gives Guidelines for the Christian to Help Him Make Proper Choices in His Conduct**
   A. Some basic considerations are: does each action please God, advance His Kingdom, or help others recognize Christ in the believer (Rom. 14:7–9) so that they might also come to faith?
   B. The believer must also consider those among the brethren who are weak. His example, while not destructive in his own life, may be calamitous in theirs. For instance, a weaker brother may become a drunkard if he sees me drinking alcoholic beverages. The question to ask is not whether it is sinful for me to do a certain thing, but how such an action will influence my weaker brother in Christ (Rom. 14:1, 21).
   C. Paul also warns us against being too quick to brand those who differ from us as wrong, and ourselves as always right (Rom. 14:2–6).
   D. We must also remember that having set a good example, we ought to be consistent with the principles of the Gospel. God will only hold us personally responsible for our own actions and motives and not for those

of others. If we influence them for good, we shall have our reward; if we influence them for evil, we shall have our corresponding condemnation (Rom. 14:10–13).

Should All Christians Agree on Everything?

Key Verses: 1 Corinthians 1:10-17

I. **God Made Us Individuals Differing One from Another**
   A. Physically God did not make us look alike. One of the greatest miracles of God is how we are all similar: one nose, two ears, two eyes, etc., and yet we are all different. We must be God's creation, for it takes God to make such infinite variety.
   B. God is also the God of spiritual individuals. We differ in the degree of our fellowship with God even though when we believe we all become children of God. As in one family, all the children belong to the same parents and are brothers and sisters among themselves, yet their relationship to one another is different, so also in the family of God. We are all children of God, and yet we are different.
   C. We must never try to hide our individuality but feel free to express it in consideration that others are different from ourselves.
   D. We should never try to make others be what we are or make ourselves what others are.
   E. The ideal is to have a healthy realistic respect for self and a proper evaluation of others. As human beings, although we are each individuals, we cannot be self-sufficient. We must live to meet the needs of others, and we must accept others as capable of meeting our needs, too. The prudent social being is one who knows how and whom to help, and how and by whom he can be helped.

II. **Where There Are Individuals, There Are Differences of Opinions**
   A. Paul is writing to believers. He calls them "brethren." One of the greatest dangers of having our individuality is to relegate the one who differs from us as a "non-brother." We certainly would not like other brothers who differ from us to consider us as not belonging to Christ.
   B. The reason for this is that our present knowledge of everything is at best partial (1 Cor. 13:9).
   C. Because our knowledge is partial, it takes the partial knowledge of many to arrive more fully at what is the whole truth of a certain matter. If only one person could think of all that could be known of a certain matter, then we would have super-minds to whom all of us would have to bow in full subjection. Society is made up of individuals complementing each other and therefore demanding mutual appreciation, which is the fiber of the happiness of group life.

III. **Can We All Speak the Same Thing without It Being Mere Repetition?**
   A. Later in 1 Corinthians 12—14 Paul delves into the problem, which apparently existed only in Corinth because of its proximity to Delphi where certain priestesses called Phythiai gave out oracular pronouncements, usually causing confusion because of their intended ambiguity. The word used in Paul's discussion about speaking in an unknown tongue, and by extension in languages other than one's native language not immediately understood by others, is the verb *laléō* from which *glōsolaliá* derives. But in 1 Corinthians 1:10 he uses another word, *légō*, which means to speak with one's understanding or *lógos*, that is, reason, intelligence. *Laléō* means either to repeat something or to say it without necessarily expressing one's own individual thought. What Paul, therefore, says here is that:

1. No Christian should become a parrot, merely repeating certain religious phrases coined by some "superhuman mind" or a superapostle (*huperlían*, 2 Cor. 11:5; 12:11).
   2. No Christian should lay aside his or her intelligence and become the blind follower of an individual who poses as a know-it-all. That was the problem in Corinth. Christians became followers of Paul, Peter, Apollos. Never arrive at the place where you say of any individual, "He knows it all and I know nothing; therefore, I am going to follow him blindly." A Christian must think for himself and make individual decisions.
  B. What is "the same thing" that Paul admonishes all Christians in Corinth to intelligently speak? The Greek expression is *tó autó* which refers to the basic truth of the Gospel. He does not refer to a phrase or a particular doctrine no matter how minor that may be. This may be termed as the Gospel which he defines in 1 Corinthians 15:1–4, ". . . that Christ died for our sins according to the Scriptures, and that he was buried, and that he rose again the third day according to the Scriptures." Anyone who does not believe that is not saved, for that is the Gospel by which we are saved (1 Cor. 15:2).

IV. Do Not Bring Schisms in the Local Body of Believers
  A. "And that there be no divisions among you." The word for "divisions" is *schísmata*, schisms. It derives from the verb *schízō*, to rip or rend and separate from the whole. The idea is that one must bear in mind that when he tears off a piece, let us say from a bed sheet, what is left behind is characterized by inadequacy, and the piece torn off can no longer serve as a sheet. If there can be fulfillment of the purpose of Christ by orderly division, that is fine; but if both parties, the one remaining and the other departing, are

hurt and made inadequate, then such a schism is improper. It should serve the basic cause of Christ.
B. Any division must not be because of a leader (vv. 12–14) or because of a particular practice such as baptism (vv. 13–17).
C. We should ask the question "When I tear apart the local body of Christ do I hurt it, do I bring harm or progress to the Gospel?"

V. What Should Characterize Believers of a Local Church?
A. After stressing the negative aspect of unity in Christ, Paul stresses the positive, ". . . that ye be perfectly joined together." The Greek verb is *ēte katērtisménoi*. The verb *katartízō* means to put together in order, to fit together like pieces of a puzzle.
  1. Paul recognizes through the use of this verb that we are all parts of a whole (1 Cor. 12:12–23). None of us can be the whole thing. It takes all of us put together to bring harmony in a chorus of varying voices. Each must sing his or her part, otherwise there can be no chorus. None of us can abdicate his part nor can we keep others from playing their part. But we must all sing in unison to reveal and exalt not ourselves but the name of Christ (v. 10).
  2. What does "perfectly" mean? Actually, the word "perfectly" is not a separate word in the Greek text. It is derived from the compound verb *katartízō* and is found in the preposition *katá*, toward or against, and the inherent meaning of the noun *ártios*, found only in 2 Timothy 3:17 and translated "perfect." It means neither faultless nor sinless, but completely capable, proficient. The compound participle would mean "cut to size in order to fit." We are to complement each other just like one piece of a puzzle is cut to fit its neighboring part.

Should All Christians Agree on Everything?

B. A Christian Mind-Set:
 1. Paul says that all the Christians' mind-sets ought to be the same. "That ye be perfectly joined together in the same mind." The word for mind is *noús* which is more of a general term indicating the whole intellect. It is that part of us which enables us to think.
 2. The mind-set of Christians is definitely different than the mind-set of unconverted people. All Christians ought to have the mind of Christ (1 Cor. 2:16). We must never evaluate Christians by the preachers they admire, but by whether they have the mind of Christ.
C. ". . . And in the same judgment": The word "judgment" in Greek is not *krísis*, but *gnốme*, opinion. It is what one thinks of a particular matter. Today, for instance, we have two predominant mind-sets, conservative and liberal, and our mind-sets determine to a great extent our individual opinions on certain particular matters. Whatever our individual opinion is on a certain matter, though it may be different somewhat from another Christian, yet it must always indicate that it is founded on the basics represented by Christ Himself. In our individual opinions we must demonstrate the mind of Christ.
D. A general rule that should govern our Christian inter-relationships is found in Romans 14:13: "Let us not therefore judge one another any more: but judge this rather, that no man put a stumbling block or an occasion to fall in his brother's way."

Two Kinds of Christians

Key Verses: 1 Corinthians 3:1-9

I. Carnal Christians
   A. Although when we become saved we are placed or baptized into Christ's body (Rom. 12:5; 1 Cor. 1:30; 12:13), we are not thereby all equally mature. In Corinth Paul recognized that many of the believers were not growing and called them "carnal" Christians. "And I, brethren could not speak unto you as unto spiritual, but as unto carnal, even as unto babes in Christ" (1 Cor. 3:1).
   B. As "babes in Christ," carnal Christians have had the new birth, but they have not grown spiritually. Therefore, these immature believers must be fed baby food as were the Corinthians (1 Cor. 3:2).
      1. The reason there is so much baby food made available to Christians today is because there are so many Christians who are just that, babies! If Christians would only grow up and work for God instead of being crybabies who only want to be fed, our world would probably experience a great spiritual revolution. The reason why so little is done for God is because babies cannot work. They just complain and cry for comfort!
      2. One treatment for carnal Christians is to feed them the solid spiritual food that they need to grow. To treat such a Christian constantly like a baby will perpetuate his or her state of immaturity. We as preachers are partially responsible for the infantile state of Christians today insofar as we have diagnosed our people as babies and have, consequently,

only given them elementary truths. The result is that our congregations remain unfruitful for Christ.

C. Carnal Christians are also those whose bodily care is their greatest concern. The Greek word for carnal is *sarkikós*, derived from *sárx*, flesh, body. Flesh is the old man in us who was crucified together with Christ when we believed (Rom. 6:6), and he remains there during our entire Christian life, raising his ugly head to claim pre-eminence over the new creation we have become through faith in Jesus Christ (2 Cor. 5:17). Even Paul sometimes felt so defeated by the old man within him that he called himself, *sarkikós* (Rom. 7:14). He diagnosed the state of the Corinthian Christians from his own experience, and we should also discern the same struggle between the flesh and spirit in ourselves.

D. Another symptom of Christian babyhood is attachment to the humans who nurture them. In Corinth, the believers became followers of Paul, Peter, Apollos, etc. We are also baby Christians if our allegiance to any human Christian leader or denomination comes before our obedient and humble attachment to Jesus Christ. Paul tried to bring the Corinthians to their senses by asking them who, after all, was crucified for them, Paul or Christ? (See 1 Cor. 1:13). Likewise, we must not put those preachers whom we see and hear closer to our hearts than Jesus who died for us and now lives, making constant intercession for us (Heb. 7:25). If we put Christ first, we will start to grow into spiritual adulthood.

E. A carnal Christian is one who places any particular doctrine or practice that distinguishes him or her from other Christians as the basis of his acceptance of and fellowship with them. Apparently, the Corinthians took pride in their baptism (1 Cor. 1:13–17). It is not through water baptism that we become brothers and sisters, but it is through our common redemption by Christ Jesus. While he chided the Corinthian Christians for being carnal babies, observe how Paul in the same breath called them brothers (1 Cor. 1:10; 2:1). Our brotherhood rests solely in our union with Jesus Christ (Eph. 4:4–6), and not in our baptism, as important as that may be.

F. The Corinthians were also filled with an attitude of spiritual superiority, which is another mark of an immature Christian. When Paul addressed them as he did in 1 Corinthians 12:1, he really intimated that they were ignorant of spiritual gifts. Similarly today, a carnal Christian learns to do something "in the flesh" then calls it a spiritual gift. This person must guard against the ensuing spiritual pride which accompanies such a work. Endeavoring to prove that one has more gifts than others is certainly a sign of spiritual babyhood.

II. Spiritual Christians

A. These believers are exactly the opposite of the carnal Christians. "And I, brethren, could not speak unto you as unto spiritual, but as unto carnal. . . ." (1 Cor. 3:1).

B. The spiritual Christian, no matter how much he accomplishes for Christ, realizes that it is God who gives the increase (1 Cor. 3:6). That verb *auxánō*, "to give increase" ("to cause to grow," NASB; to "make things grow," NIV) is very important for us to understand in 1 Corinthians 3:6. It is growth which is brought about by a factor or a cause other than oneself. A seed is placed in the ground, it is watered, and it grows. In the regularity of the experience, we are tempted to conclude that there is self-generation. But it is not so. We must always recognize that it is God who puts life into the seed, and it is God who makes it grow. A manmade seed with all the same constituent parts, placed in the ground and watered, will never grow. A spiritual Christian is one who recognizes and bows to God's power in all of the demonstrations of life. He recognizes that he is the zero after the one and that without the one coming first, he will always be a zero.

C. A mature Christian is one who never considers himself as having arrived. He is constantly growing; the moment he stops growing he is reverting to the status of carnality. In 1 Corinthians 3:9 there is a word translated "building." It is *oikodomē,* which means a building in the process of being constructed. "For we are laborers together with God: . . . ye are God's building." He never finishes with us till our last breath. When we allow Him to keep on building us, we are spiritual. Interestingly enough, *oikodomē* is the same Greek word used in 2 Corinthians 5:1 to represent our eternal house in the heavens. The quality of our home in heaven will be determined by the quality of our lives as Christians on earth. What better incentive could we have to become less carnal and more spiritual!

D. What kind of Christian are you—a carnal or a spiritual Christian?

The Purpose of Pentecost

Key Verses: 1 Corinthians 12:3-13

I. Pentecost Is Rooted in the Old Testament and Fulfilled in the New Testament
   A. The Greek *Pentēkostē* is actually an adjective with the word *hēméra*, "day," implied after it. It was celebrated on the "fiftieth day" after the First Fruits Festival of the Jews and was the second of the three chief Hebrew holy days (Lev. 23:9–21). In the Old Testament, Pentecost was called "the feast of harvest, the firstfruits of thy labors" (Ex. 23:16).
   B. In the New Testament Pentecost is mentioned in three places: Acts 2:1; 20:16; and 1 Corinthians 16:8. It occurred on the fiftieth day after Easter, which itself coincides with the Feast of First Fruits. Christ's resurrection thus represents the first fruits of all those to follow (1 Cor. 15:23). Then on Pentecost with the coming of the Holy Spirit, the Church was initiated. Just as in the Old Testament, the Feast of Pentecost celebrated the beginning of the harvest.
   C. From Acts 20:16 we infer that Pentecost must have been part of the early Christian calendar, since Paul earnestly desired to present the gifts of the Gentile churches to the saints in Judea at Pentecost. By the close of the Second Century it appeared as one of the established celebrations of the Church.
   D. In more recent times it has also been called Whitsunday. In the English church the Pentecost season was especially used for baptisms. From the white robes worn by the candidates, the term "Whitsunday" is supposed to have arisen.

II. Pentecost Marks the Special Descent of the Holy Spirit, Yet He Exists Eternally and Works as Part of the Triune God

A. In Hebrews 9:14 we have all three personalities mentioned, "How much more shall the blood of Christ, who through the eternal Spirit ['eternal,' *aiōnios*, ascribes death and timelessness] offered himself without spot to God [in Greek 'the God' meaning 'the Father'], purge your conscience from dead works to serve the living God [without the article indicating the unity of the Trinity]."

B. Just as Jesus Christ came into the world through the Holy Spirit (Luke 1:35; Matt. 1:18, 20), so also the Holy Spirit was first manifested in the form of a dove which descended upon Jesus at His baptism (Matt. 3:16; Mark 1:10; Luke 3:22) and affirmed His messianic office. This appearance indicates that the Holy Spirit existed prior to Pentecost. He is also mentioned in the Old Testament (Gen. 1:2; Job 26:13; Is. 32:15). But even as Jesus Christ existed as the eternal Logos (John 1:1) and came into the world (John 1:10–14) to be objectively observed, so also did the Holy Spirit appear for the sake of mankind at Pentecost (Acts 2:1–13) and on various subsequent occasions to both Jews and Gentiles (Acts 11:14–18; 10:44–46; 19:1–7).

C. This special coming of the Holy Spirit had been prophesied by the Lord Jesus (John 14:16, 17; 16:7–15). In John 7:37–39 Jesus spoke metaphorically of how the Holy Spirit would fill the believer. Then in verse 39 an editorial explanation is given linking Jesus' comments to the future coming of the Spirit, "But this spake He of the Spirit, which they that believe on Him should receive: for the Holy Ghost was not yet given; because that Jesus was not yet glorified."

III. The Advent of the Holy Spirit Accomplished Many Objectives in the Church

A. At Pentecost the Holy Spirit poured out His power upon the church (Acts 1:5, 8; 2:1–13).

B. The Holy Spirit also gives gifts to each believer for the purpose of building up the church (1 Cor. 12:4–11; Eph. 4:11, 12).

C. He miraculously and mystically unites each believer of the past, present and future into the body of Christ. This truth is clearly taught in 1 Corinthians 12:13, "For by ['in,' *en*, by means of] one Spirit are we all baptized into one body, whether we be Jews or Gentiles, whether we be bond or free; and have been all [*pántes*, each one individually and all as a unit] made to drink into one Spirit." Note that Paul uses the same metaphor of drinking that Jesus does in John 7:37–39.

D. It is the Holy Spirit who directs us to drink of the water of life offered by Jesus and thus become part of His body (John 16:13). The church is composed of all the Old Testament saints who looked forward to the coming of Jesus, all New Testament saints who put their trust in Christ, and even the Tribulation saints yet to come.

What Guarantee Do We Have That We Shall Be Raised from the Dead?

Key Verses: 1 Corinthians 15:20-28

I. Can We Trust a Philosophical Presupposition Over a Proven Fact?
   A. The philosophical presupposition among some of the Corinthians was that there could be no resurrection from the dead (1 Cor. 15:12).
   B. Could we hold to such a presupposition if it could be proven that someone who lived on earth actually did rise from the dead?
   C. Paul attempts to prove that very fact of history to the Corinthians in his first letter to them.
      1. He lists those who saw the resurrected Christ, ending with himself (1 Cor. 15:3–9).
      2. Next he offers what we call *ad absurdum* arguments. Suppose there is no resurrection of the dead. Then Jesus never rose. And if so, Paul's preaching was empty as was the faith of the Corinthian believers. He and all others who preach the Gospel should be declared false witnesses. Those who died are lost forever, and those who are alive are miserable (vv. 12–19).
   D. Then follows the greatest declaration we have in Paul's writings, "But now is Christ risen from the dead, and become the firstfruits of them that slept" (1 Cor. 15:20). "But now" *nuní*, introduces a contrast. It stands in antithesis to something done in times past. Because

of the historical resurrection of Christ, things in the future are going to be different than before. *Nuní* is used similarly in Romans 3:21; 6:22; 1 Corinthians 5:11 and Philemon 1:11. It is as if Paul were saying: "From now on you can look at death differently because Christ has conquered death." The fact wins out over the presupposition.

II. **What Was Involved in Christ's Resurrection?**
   A. The verb that is used in 1 Corinthians 15:20 is *egēgertai*, "to raise himself." While in both the NASB and NIV the verb is passive, "has been raised," in the KJV it is translated "is risen." It really should be "raised himself." Christ being God on earth, could do just that. In unequivocal terms Jesus predicted His power to do so when He said in John 2:19, "Destroy this temple" (referring to His body), "and in three days I will raise it up." In John 10:17, 18, Jesus also claimed power to take up His life again. In fact, the chief priests and Pharisees accused Jesus of having claimed deity by declaring that He was going to raise Himself from the dead. No man had ever made such a claim before. He even fixed the time of His resurrection—in three days—and He did it!
   B. Other passages of Scripture say that God the Father was also responsible for raising Jesus from the dead (Gal. 1:1; Eph. 1:19, 20).
   C. Jesus not only rose from the dead, but He is still alive today. This fact is indicated by the perfect tense *egēgertai*, referring to a past event, the results of which continue. This cannot be said of any other person. Those who were raised died again, but Jesus rose and lives on.

III. **Christ's Resurrection Is the Guarantee of Ours Yet to Come**
   A. Christ is called the firstfruits, *aparchē*, "one making a start" (1 Cor. 15:20). This term indicates that there were none before, but that there will be many to follow. We see the first fruit on the tree, and then we know that there will be more of the same kind.
   B. Death, for the Christian, is likened to sleep (1 Cor. 15:51). It is the body, however, not the soul, which sleeps at death. The dead body is like a seed placed in the ground. The seed itself dies, but from it springs new life. The plant is different from the seed and yet continues its identity. So shall it be for the believer at the final resurrection (1 Cor. 15:36, 42–49).

How to Be Reconciled to God

Key Verses: 2 Corinthians 5:16-21

I. **Unsaved Man Is Now at Enmity with God**
   A. The Bible tells us bluntly that sinners are "enemies" of God (Rom. 5:10; Col. 1:21; James 4:4).
      1. They chose to reject God in Adam, their representative (Rom. 5:12).
      2. Romans 3:23 tells us that "All have sinned, and come short of the glory of God."
         a) God has no capricious enmity against man. It is the result of man's rejection of God. This wrath of God is one that springs from love (John 3:16).
         b) In his present fallen state, man cannot recognize who God really is—that He is a loving Father waiting for the return of His prodigal son (Luke 15:11–32).
         c) Glory, *dóxa*, comes from *dokéō*, to recognize. Man cannot recognize God's earnest desire for him.
      3. The word "wrath" in Greek is *orgḗ*, a state of mind, in contrast to *thumós*, anger, which is an outburst of that state of mind with the purpose of revenge. Actually *orgḗ* derives from *orégomai*, to desire eagerly or earnestly. Aristotle says *orgḗ*, wrath, is a desire with grief (see Mark 3:5). God, in His estrangement from man, experiences not only wrath but deep grief.

How to Be Reconciled to God

II. God's Love Plus His Justice Brings Wrath with Grief
   A. God created man in His image and likeness, that is, with the capability of choice. He gave man a unique spirit with which to choose.
   B. He prefixed the consequences of man's choice. Obedience would have meant eternal friendship with God, but disobedience would bring disruption of that friendship.
   C. Man chose to disobey God. What was God to do? He had already declared the punishment of such disobedience. Had He not kept His word, He would have proven Himself unreliable. He did what we as loving parents do when our children disobey us. We punish them, not because we do not love them, but because we do and we want to correct them. If we state that we are going to punish them but don't do it, chaos will result.

III. God's Initiative to Reconcile Us to Himself
   A. Unlike our estrangement from God, our reconciliation to God was initiated by Him.
   B. The word which describes the bridging between God and man in the New Testament is "reconciliation." The Greek word is *katallagē*. It is found only in Paul's writings (Rom. 5:11; 11:15; 2 Cor. 5:18).
      1. The verb *katallássō* is similarly found only in Paul's writings (Rom. 5:10; 1 Cor. 7:11; 2 Cor. 5:18–20). There is also the compound verb *apokatallássō* (only in Eph. 2:16; Col. 1:20, 21, from *apó*, from, *katá*, an intensive and *allássō*, to change). The compound *apokatallássō* has more of the sense of the acceptance of the restored person by God.
      2. Second Corinthians 5:17 describes this change, "If any man be in Christ he is a new creature: old things are passed away; behold, all things are become new."

    a) The word for "new" is *kainé* which means qualitatively new.
    b) When man accepts God's provision for his reconciliation to Him, He makes him a new creation. From an enemy He makes man a friend. This is the miracle of man's salvation.
  3. Lest there be a misunderstanding as to who caused this change, we have the statement in 2 Corinthians 5:18, "And all things are of God."
    a) The preposition "of" is *ek*, out of God. He took the initiative and He accomplished the reconciliation.
    b) The article *toú* is in front of *Theoú*, God, which indicates the Father. It is He, God the Father, who reconciled us.
    c) The translation "who hath reconciled us to himself" is unfortunate for it gives the idea that it is Christ who is referred to.
    d) The verb is in the aorist participle which refers to the historical event of what Christ did once and for all. It is *toú katalláxantos*, "who [God the Father] did reconcile us to himself through Jesus Christ. . . ."
    e) Christ did what needed to be done to satisfy the Father's justice, paying that proper punishment for our sins. Christ shed His blood, and is, therefore, able to cleanse us from all sin, making us new creatures in Him.

IV. **Man's Acceptance of God's Provision for Reconciliation**
  A. In order for man once again to become God's friend, it is necessary for sinful man to accept Christ's work on the cross. This is called believing in Christ.
  B. "He that believeth on Him [Christ] is not condemned . . ." (John 3:18). The old judgment is an-

nulled. Christ was judged on behalf of sinful man. And then we read, "but he that believeth not is condemned already because he hath not believed in the name of the only begotten Son of God" (John 3:18). This is the old condemnation not removed, and if not removed, remains as part and parcel of man.

The Blessing of Suffering

Key Verses: Philippians 3:8-14

I. The Christian and Suffering
   A. All suffering of the entire mankind is the consequence of man's original sin.
      1. Romans 5:12 clearly states that death, which is the ultimate suffering, came through sin upon all men.
      2. As there are general blessings for all people, believers and unbelievers alike (Matt. 5:45), so there are general sufferings shared by believers and unbelievers.
         a) Unbelievers bear suffering by themselves, for God does not share in their sufferings. But believers share Christ's suffering, and He shares in theirs. Thus, although God may not directly ordain suffering, He uses it and turns it into a blessing, even as Christ's suffering became a blessing to mankind.
         b) Philippians 1:29 makes this point clear when studied in the Greek text: "For unto you it is given in the behalf of Christ, not only to believe on Him, but also to suffer for His sake." The phrase "it is given" in Greek is *echarísthē*, which is derived from the words *cháris*, grace, and *chárisma*, gift. Two things constitute God's gifts to us as Christians: to believe in Christ and to suffer for Him. Therefore, as salvation is a gift of His grace, so also is suffering.
   B. Paul's desire expressed in Philippians 3:10 was "to know him, and the power of his resurrection, and the

fellowship of his sufferings, being made conformable unto his death."
1. Suffering cannot be a blessing unless one has first partaken of the power of Christ's resurrection, that is, becoming a new creature in Christ Jesus.
2. If suffering is a curse, that person needs to be born again and experience Christ's resurrection.
3. Christ promised His disciples that they were going to experience tribulation, but they would have inner peace as they experienced it (John 16:33).
4. Believers in the New Testament are never said to be exempt from suffering.
    a) Paul suffered and was mistreated at Philippi (1 Thess. 2:2). There he endured stripes and imprisonment (Acts 16:19ff.). He also suffered because of the perverse ideas of his converts (1 Cor. 9:12; 2 Cor. 1:6).
    b) The Galatians suffered many things (Acts 14:2–5; 19–22).
    c) The Philippians suffered on behalf of Christ (Phil. 1:29).
    d) The Thessalonians suffered for the kingdom of God (2 Thess. 1:4, 5) at the hands of their fellow countrymen, as also the churches of Judea at the hands of the Jews (1 Thess. 2:14).
    e) The recipients of First Peter were also subjected to suffering. They suffered wrongfully for well-doing (1 Pet. 2:19, 20), for righteousness' sake (3:14, 17), as Christians (4:16). Peter said that those who are called to God's eternal kingdom in Christ would suffer (5:10), just as Paul had told Timothy that "all that would live godly in Christ Jesus shall suffer persecution" (2 Tim. 3:12).
    f) Among things which the Christians at Smyrna had to suffer was imprisonment (Rev. 2:10).

g) The Hebrews are reminded that after they were enlightened they "endured a great conflict of sufferings; partly being made a gazing stock both by reproaches and by afflictions; and partly, becoming partakers with them that were so used" (Heb. 10:32, 33).

h) The heroes suffered for their faithfulness. Moses prepared to suffer affliction with the people of God (Heb. 11:25).

i) The prophets also gave an example of suffering (James 5:10).

j) Our concern as Christians should be to suffer according to the will of God (1 Pet. 3:17; 4:19), that is, for well-doing.

II. The Fruits of Suffering for the Christian

A. Christ, as the first fruits of our suffering, because of His suffering of death, was crowned with glory and honor (Heb. 2:9).
   1. Glory followed His sufferings (1 Pet. 1:11).
   2. Through sufferings, He became perfect, that is, He reached the goal for which He became man (Heb. 2:10; cf. 5:8).

B. In the case of His followers, suffering has a similar result. Those who suffer for righteousness' sake are blessed, *makárioi* (1 Pet. 3:14).
   1. Those who are called to God's eternal glory in Christ and suffer a while shall be perfected (reach their God-intended goal), established, and strengthened by God (1 Pet. 5:10).
   2. One who suffers as a Christian has reason to glorify God and cause Him to be recognized in his or her life (1 Pet. 4:16).
   3. To do well and to suffer for it is acceptable with Him (1 Pet. 2:20; 4:19).

III. How Can We Have Fellowship in Christ's Sufferings?
   A. The presence of sin in the lives of people made Christ suffer.
   B. For their sins, He bore the cross. This was unique with Him. We cannot redemptively suffer for others, but we can sorrow in the presence of their sins, witness and pray.
   C. Although Christ died for the sins of others, He did not choose to enforce His salvation.
   D. He wept over Jerusalem (Matt. 23:37–39; Luke 13:34, 35). We must weep over what refuses to change in response to His grace and our witness of it. This is the demonstration of mercy by us.
   E. He suffered when He saw people not knowing the wrongness of what they were doing. With what agony He must have cried from the cross: "Father, forgive them, for they know not what they do." They thought they were harming Jesus by putting Him to death, but in reality they were instruments in God's hands in executing His plan of redemption.

How to Be an Example Worth Following

Key Verses: Philippians 3:17—4:1

I. **The First Part of Philippians 3:17 Constitutes a Commandment by Paul**
   A. The word translated "followers" in 1 Corinthians 11:1 is *mimētaí mou*, the plural of *mimētḗs*, imitator.
      1. As an adjectival noun it occurs in 1 Corinthians 4:16; 11:1; Ephesians 5:1; 1 Thessalonians 1:6; 2:14; Hebrews 6:12.
      2. It means, "Observe what I say and what I do and you do likewise; follow my example."
      3. It implies that Paul's example is worth following.
      4. In order to be able to say this to fellow Christians, one must be careful that he or she does not set one's self and one's peculiarities, which we all have, as the standard for others to follow.
      5. We must be careful lest when we say, "Follow me," that we do not desire to set ourselves up as little messiahs, little christs or gods.
      6. Such were in Corinth, those Paul called *huperlían apóstoloi*, or great superapostles (2 Cor. 11:5). Unfortunately the KJV gives room for misinterpretation by calling them "chief apostles." The NKJV missed it by calling them "most eminent apostles." The NIV caught the meaning accurately when it calls them "superapostles." There were false apostles who set themselves up as the standard, and they demanded that what they taught be followed, regardless of agreement or disagreement with the teaching of Christ who must be set as the absolute standard.

How to Be an Example Worth Following

B. Here in Philippians 3:17 the Greek word is *summimetaí mou*.
   1. The KJV translates it thus: "Be followers together with me."
   2. The NIV, "Join with others in following my example."
   3. The NKJV translates it: "Join in following my example" which is closest to the meaning.
   4. The word *summimetés*, occurring only in Philippians 3:17, is not the same as *mimetés*, an imitator. The preposition *sún* means together, that is, with Paul. First Corinthians 11:1 declares "Be ye followers [*mimetaí*—imitators] of me, even as I also am of Christ." What Paul meant is, "Together with me, you imitate Christ." Another way to put it is: "In the proportion that I imitate Christ, you imitate me."
      a) He stresses that he, as a human being, is not worthy of imitation.
      b) But because he was an imitator of Christ he was worthy of imitation.
      c) It is the same as saying, "Imitate that which you see in me, but only insofar as you discern it as being Christ in me."
      d) The word *summimetaí*, imitators together or with, must have as an object not Paul but Christ. Be imitators together with me of Christ. Let us both imitate Christ. The word "Christ" in the genitive is to be understood although it is not actually there. It is the same as 1 Corinthians 11:1, "Even as I am of Christ."

II. In What Was Paul an Imitator of Christ?
   A. "Wherefore I beseech you, be ye followers of me" (1 Cor. 4:16). The correct translation is "Be my imitators," *mimetaí*.

1. Carefully study 1 Corinthians 4. It delineates the easy affluent life of the Corinthians and the contrasting sacrificial life of the Apostles.
2. The sum total is: My life of sacrifice should be an imitation of the life of Christ, which is worth following. There is more joy in sacrifice than in selfish enrichment.

B. "Be ye followers [imitators] of me, even as I also am of Christ" (1 Cor. 11:1). What are the things Paul brings out in this chapter?
1. He delivered to the Corinthians without any change the teaching that he had received from Christ (1 Cor. 11:2).
2. Therefore, this teaching should remain unaltered by the Corinthians and all the subsequent generations of Christians. Christ's teaching must always remain as taught by Him and delivered by the original apostles of Christ.
    a) The teaching concerned the structure of the family. The head is Christ; the head of the wife is the husband (v. 3). A couple makes up one body, one flesh (Matt. 19:5), and there can be only one head on one body. If there are two, then the oneness in marriage is missing.
    b) Christ's sacrifice on the cross ought to be remembered through the ordinance of the Lord's Supper (vv. 20–29). We should dwell more on the magnitude of Christ's sacrifice for us than boast of our insignificant work for Him.

C. "And ye became followers [*mimētaí*, imitators] of us and of the Lord, having received the word in much affliction with joy of the Holy Ghost" (1 Thess. 1:6). Paul commends the Thessalonian believers in that they had already followed his example in rejoicing in affliction (2 Cor. 11:21–33).

How to Be an Example Worth Following

    1. Their affliction ought to be considered not as being a result of spiritual disobedience, but as God's own way of making them partners with Christ's sufferings (Phil. 1:12; 2:29; 3:10; James 1:2–4).
    2. This affliction resulting from Christ's righteousness in us is only temporary since Christ is coming to liberate us from the great tribulation (Matt. 24:21; 1 Thess. 1:10; 4:15–17; 2 Thess. 1:7).
  D. "For ye brethren, became followers of the churches of God which in Judea are in Christ Jesus: for ye also have suffered like things of your own countrymen, even as they have of the Jews" (1 Thess. 2:14). As Paul suffered beating by the Jews (2 Cor. 11:24), so must we expect the worst treatment by those of our own nation, community and family (Matt. 10:34–37).

III. Evaluate Others
  A. The second commandment in Philippians 3:17 is: "Mark them which walk so as ye have us for an example."
  B. Positively identify the imitators of Christ and of me, Paul was saying. You need their fellowship.
  C. Only secondarily mark those who do not follow Christ and Paul.
    1. Paul calls such "the enemies of the cross of Christ" (Phil. 3:18).
    2. They are so called because they were teaching, as many are today, that the cross in the Christian life ought to be avoided instead of welcomed. They were teaching that prosperity and wealth alone are to be sought as blessings, but not the inevitable sufferings of the cross of Christ.
    3. Association with those who look upon material possessions as an indispensable blessing of the believer in Christ is to be shunned. Such are to be

marked and recognized for what they are: "enemies of the cross of Christ" whose punishment is clearly delineated in Philippians 3:19, while the believer's hope is the incorruptible body of the resurrection (Rom. 8:23; Phil. 3:20, 21).

The Resources and Responsibilities of the Believer

Key Verses: Colossians 1:9-11

I. **The Believer's Faith Grows by Doing**
   A. At conversion we acquire the ability to receive God's revelation, but that does not mean that God gives us complete knowledge. For that reason, Paul prays continually for being filled "with the knowledge of his will" (Col. 1:9).
   B. In Colossians 1:10 Paul speaks of this knowledge (*epígnōsis*) as increasing, "That ye might walk worthy of the Lord unto all pleasing, being fruitful in every good work, and increasing in the knowledge of God."
   C. Having the life of Christ in us proves itself in our desire to fulfill the conditions of growth and maturity. We are to work out our own salvation with fear and trembling (Phil. 2:12). It is only as we are fruitful that we increase. It is only as we serve others that we grow in the Lord. Observe how the two verbs occur together in Colossians 1:10, being "fruitful" and "increasing."
   D. The genuineness of salvation is to be found in the fruitfulness of the seed that falls in the human heart, as is so ably demonstrated by our Lord in the parable of the sower. The same verb, *karpophoréō*, to bring forth fruit, that is used in Colossians 1:10 is also used in that parable in its three occurrences: Matthew 13:23; Mark 4:20; and Luke 8:15. Without fruitfulness, faith is dead (James 2:14–26).

E. The fruit that salvation brings is described in Galatians 5:22, 23, whereas the contrasting fruit of the flesh is set forth in Galatians 5:19–21.

II. Paul Portrays the Responsibilities of the Believer in Colossians 1:10

A. Because Christ is in us, we must be careful to "walk worthy of the Lord" and never embarrass Him by the choices we make.

B. The verb "walk" is in the aorist infinitive in the Greek, indicating a series of individual steps that we take. We must examine our life step by step instead of averaging it out on the whole to discover if we are pleasing to the Lord.

C. The word for "Lord" is *kúrios*, meaning absolute master. Is He the total Lord of our lives, or do we seek to have our own way from time to time?

D. Paul adds, "unto all pleasing." The NASB says "in all respects" and the NIV, "in every way." The Greek expression is *eis pásan areskeían* meaning "that you may fully please the Lord." The word *aréskeia*, is only found here in the entire New Testament and means desire of pleasing, emphasizing the close attention God gives our lives. What is translated "unto all," *pásan*, is really an adjective conveying the idea of full satisfaction. We are greatly tempted in the Christian walk to do things only for the partial satisfaction of God while fully pleasing ourselves the rest of the time. If the Lord is not fully satisfied, He may not be satisfied at all.

E. Next is added, in "every good work." The adjective for "good" is *agathós*, which means benevolent. God is fully satisfied when our works stem from a benevolent concern for others.

What Is Reconciliation?

Key Verses: Colossians 1:20-29

I. The Meaning of Reconciliation
   A. In English, the verb means to conciliate, to unite again, to bring back into harmony. It does not necessarily imply change in the character of either or both parties. Neither may acknowledge fault, but rather choose to simply tolerate each other.
   B. In Greek, however, there are three words used to differentiate the various changes which may occur.
      1. First, there is the verb *dialássō*, used in Matthew 5:24, where we are told to reconcile ourselves to someone who has something against us. Usually in such a case there is fault on both sides, but the offending party must take the initiative to restore the relationship. *Dialássō* is derived from the preposition *diá*, through, and *allássō*, to change. Thus, there is a definite change which must take place in either one or both of the parties before they can be reconciled.
      2. Next, the verb *katallássō* is used to show the reconciliation which takes place between God and man (Rom. 5:10; 2 Cor. 5:18–20). In this case, the reason for the estrangement is clearly man's disobedience and fall in Adam (Rom. 5:12–14). In order to be restored, man must acknowledge his sin and believe that through Christ's death he can be reconciled to God (Acts 2:38; 2 Cor. 5:18). The verb *katallássō* is made up of the intensive *katá*, meaning completely, and *allássō*, to change. Jesus describes

this complete change as being "born again" (John 3:3) and Paul as becoming "a new creature" (2 Cor. 5:17). Only by such a conversion can man once again become acceptable to God (Rom. 5:1).
3. A third word, *apokatallássō*, is also used in Scripture to describe man's complete restoration to his former position before the fall (Eph. 2:16; Col. 1:20, 21). Unfortunately, this verb is translated by the same English word as *katallássō*, reconcile. The additional preposition *apó*, however, means that the reconciliation is carried a step further from friendship with God to a reinstatement as sons (Rom. 8:15–17).

II. Believers Are Thus Restored in a State of Privilege
A. The intimacy of our renewed relationship with Christ is indicated by the metaphor of the body (Eph. 2:16; 1 Cor. 12:1ff.). Christ is described as the head, and we as members of His body (Eph. 1:22; 4:15; 5:23). Our status, however, is a tremendous responsibility as well as a privilege. When any other member hurts, we must also hurt (1 Cor. 12:26), and we are commanded to "Bear ye one another's burdens, and so fulfill the law of Christ" (Gal. 6:2).
B. The day is coming when Christ will restore everything to Himself including the creation (Col. 1:20; Rom. 8:19–23) and even our mortal bodies (1 Cor. 15:52).
C. Greatest of all, we will truly become saints (*hágioi*), spotless, "unblameable and unreproveable in His sight" (Col. 1:22).

Spiritual Garments Befitting the Christian

Key Verses: Colossians 3:12-17

I. To Live the Christian Life We Must Put Off the Garments of the Old Man
   A. Paul tells us in Colossians 3:8, 9, "But now ye also put off all these: anger, wrath, malice, blasphemy, filthy communication out of your mouth. Lie not one to another, seeing that ye have put off the old man with his deeds."
   B. Paul's admonition warns us that our old nature must still be dealt with in this life. The two verbs translated "put off" in these two verses are not the same. The one in verse 8 is *apothésthe*, the aorist imperative of *apotíthēmi*, meaning "distance away from oneself." These sins of our old life will try to seduce us. Because Christ put them to death on the cross (Rom. 6:6), however, we now have the power in our lives to overcome them. But the actual job of distancing ourselves from them is ours, not Christ's.
   C. Before we were saved, we could not separate ourselves from sin because these sins were a very part of our own sinful nature. The verb to "put off" used in verse 9 is *apekdusámenoi*, the aorist participle of the verb *apekdúō*, "to put a garment away from you." This garment represents our sinful nature which must be removed before we are able to resist sinning. If we will reckon ourselves dead to sin as Paul commands in Romans 6:11 because of our identification with Christ (Col. 3:3), then we will have the power to dis-

tance ourselves from the individual sins mentioned in verses 8 and 9.

II. Putting Off the Old Man is Not Enough; We Must Put On the New Man as Well

A. In verse 10 we have the Greek word *enthusámenoi*, from the verb, *endúō*, "to dress one's self," which is the exact opposite of *ekdúō*, "to put off one's garments" used in verse 9. Because the Christian is one who has the divine as well as the sinful nature in himself (2 Pet. 1:4), there is a personal undressing and dressing to do. The aorist participle of these two verbs is used, indicative of a once and for all undressing and dressing. We must consider whose we are, mortify our old nature (Col. 3:5), and set our affection on things above (Col. 3:2).

B. When we come to verse 12 we again have the verb *endúsasthe*, the aorist imperative of *endúō*, "to dress ourselves with." These characteristics of the new man are actually to be put on and made a very part of ourselves so that the outer man might match the desires of the new inner man. In Romans 7, Paul describes the constant struggle he had to conform his outer life to his inner desires. Here he describes it as a daily dressing with Christ-like qualities.

III. What Do Our New Clothes Look Like?

A. First, we shall put on "bowels of mercies" (v. 12). The word for bowels is *spláchna*, akin to *splēn*, "spleen," from which the Greeks believed emanated man's inner disposition. That is where mercy begins, inside man. The word used here for mercy is *oiktirmós*, not *éleos*, the common word for mercy. The meaning of *oiktirmós* is to have compassion in an active manner, as well as an inner sympathy (*éleos*). Thus the Christian must have an inner feeling of pity which outwardly mani-

fests itself in helping the object of mercy.
B. Next, slip into "kindness" (v. 12), *chrestótēs*, which means that grace which pervades the whole nature, mellowing all which would have been harsh and austere. In Galatians 5:22 the word *chrestótēs* is rendered "gentleness" and precedes *agathosúnē*, "goodness." The first is passive, indicating character, and the other indicates active benevolence. Gentleness would be a closer translation of *chrestótēs* here as well. We may not always be able to help others, but we must always show the gentle spirit of Christ in us.
C. We must also cover ourselves with "humility," (v. 12) *tapeinophrosúnē*, in the KJV translated "humbleness of mind." The Greek word is derived from *tapeinós*, "one who recognizes his true condition," and *phrónēma*, "mind set." The compound actually means the set of mind that correctly estimates one's true worth in being and possessions. We should, therefore, recognize those above us, whose help we need, as well as those below us, who need our help.
D. Paul next mentions "meekness," from the Greek word *praótēs*, which according to Aristotle is the virtue which stands between *aorgēsía*, "not showing any anger or wrath when justified" and *orgelótēs*, "being angry without cause." Contrary to popular opinion, "meekness," involves getting angry for the right reason, at the right time, and in the right measure, as demonstrated by our Lord (Mark 3:5).
E. Another Christian virtue we must acquire is "long-suffering," (v. 12) *makrothumía*. Unlike "patience," *hupomonḗ*, which is a passive attitude, "long-suffering" involves actively trying to win others to Christ without discouragements.
F. This attitude is closely related to the next one Paul mentions in verse 13, "forbearing," from *anechómenoi*, which means "tolerating or putting up with." The fol-

lowing expression "one another" is *allḗlōn*, which derives from *állos*, "another of the same kind." Others are the "same kind" as we are. Just as they must tolerate our imperfections, we must put up with theirs also.

G. "Forbearing" is connected to "forgiving one another" (v. 13), meaning *charizómenoi heautoís*, meaning "yourselves forgiving." Notice that a different Greek word for "one another" is used here. It is *heautoís*, "in your very own selves." The verb, *charizómenoi*, means "providing grace" and is not the usual verb for "forgive," *aphíemi*, or "put away from." Just as Christ extended His own grace toward us, causing our redemption so we must put under grace the sins against us done by others.

H. Lastly, Paul tells us to surround ourselves with "charity" the crowning garment of the new man in Christ (Col. 3:14). The Greek word for "charity" or "love" is *agápē*, which is that type of love that considers others in light of what we can do for them and not what they can do for us. Such love "is the bond of perfectness," holding all the other virtues of the Christian life together so they can reach their divinely intended goal *teleiótēs*. Without love, all the other attributes that we display will contribute nothing to the glory of God.

Paul's Work among the Thessalonians Was Short but Effective

Key Verses: 1 Thessalonians 2:1-8

I. If I Am a Preacher, My Ministry Must Count for Christ
   A. What a joy it must have been for Paul in writing to the Thessalonians to say to them, "For yourselves, brethren, know our entrance in unto you, that it was not in vain" (1 Thess. 2:1). The word for "in vain" is *kenē*, "empty, accomplished nothing." Preaching must accomplish something, or otherwise it is empty.
   B. Paul's ministry was effective in that those to whom he preached "believed" (1 Thess. 2:10).

II. In Acts 17:1-9, Luke Describes Paul's Brief but Successful Ministry in Thessalonica
   A. As was his custom, Paul first went to the synagogue where it was natural to find God-fearing people (Acts 17:1, 2).
   B. He then presented the Gospel to them in an intelligent manner, ". . . reasoned with them out of the Scriptures (Acts 17:2). The verb for "reasoned" is *dielégeto*, the imperfect of *dialégomai*, which derives from *diá*, "through" and *légō*, "to speak intelligently." It is the word from which the English word dialectic comes, that branch of logic which teaches the art of logically discerning the truth. This method of preaching was used by Paul in Athens (Acts 17:17), in Corinth (Acts 18:4), in Ephesus (Acts 18:19; 19:8), in Troas (Acts 20:7, 9), and also before Felix (Acts 24:25).

C. Paul taught at the synagogue for only three Sabbaths. Here is a church established as a result of preaching three times.
D. His messages were "out of the Scriptures" (Acts 17:2), and they presented the "gospel of God" (1 Thess. 2:2). This "gospel" included the necessary death and resurrection of Christ (Acts 17:3). He identified Jesus as the anointed of God in spite of the fact he knew that it would cause the Jews to hate him (Acts 17:5).
E. Not all believed, but some did (Acts 17:4).
F. Disturbance and persecution arose, but the Church of the Thessalonians was firmly established. Paul's ministry, although short and turbulent, was successful.

III. **In His Letter Paul Pinpoints the Effective Characteristics of His Ministry in Thessalonica**
  A. First of all, Paul spoke boldly: ". . . we were bold in our God to speak unto you the gospel of God . . ." (v. 2). The verb in Greek is *parrēsiázomai*, "to speak boldly, to be free, frank, bold in speech, demeanor, action," and is characteristic of Paul's preaching (Acts 9:27, 29; 13:46; 14:3; 18:26; 19:8; and Eph. 6:20). This boldness took real effort on Paul's part. In verse 2 the Greek word *agṓn* translated "contention" (KJV) should be rendered with "great struggle." As in Paul's case, a preacher should expect great struggle internally, as well as externally, when he speaks out boldly for Christ.
  B. Secondly, Paul taught the truth (v. 3). The word "exhortation" is *paráklēsis*, literally meaning "a calling near" as in Acts 13:15 and 15:30.
    1. Some teaching of the Word of God according to Paul, can be "of deceit" instead of bringing us nearer to God.
    2. In verse 3 he also mentions teaching "of uncleanness," referring to teaching that justifies moral sin. *Akatharsía*, translated "uncleanness," refers to lewd-

ness as opposed to chastity (Rom. 1:24; 6:19; 2 Cor. 12:21; Gal. 5:19; Eph. 4:19; 5:3; Col. 3:5; 1 Thess. 4:7). We should also examine the lifestyle of the preacher, as well as his instruction, on the subject of purity (1 Tim. 3:2 and Titus 1:6) before giving him credence.

    3. Teaching can also be done in a fraudulent way, *en dólō*, "in guile." The preposition used here is *en*, "in" or "by means of," and the noun is *dólos* derived from *délear*, "bait." False teachers will bait us with watered down truths in order to attract us to their own incorrect teaching. On the other hand, in our Lord there was never *dólos*, "guile," in His mouth (1 Pet. 2:22).

C. Paul indicates that he was not a man-pleaser: ". . . not as pleasing men, but God . . ." (v. 4).

D. Neither did he use flattery. "For neither at any time used we flattering words. . . ." Paul, instead, challenged his listeners to live a more godly life.

E. Paul did not have selfish motives for his teaching ". . . nor a cloak of covetousness" (v. 5). What is translated "a cloak" is *próphasis*, "a pretext, an excuse." A Bible teacher should not find pretexts for acquiring material wealth from the people to whom he ministers.

F. Another thing Paul did not do was to seek glory or recognition from men (v. 6).

G. Far from being a burden (v. 6), Paul actually supported himself during his ministry.

H. Paul was *hḗpios*, translated "gentle" in 1 Thessalonians 2:7, as opposed to being a fighter, described in 2 Timothy 2:24, "And the servant of the Lord must not strive" (*máchesthai*, "to fight as if in war or in battle").

I. Lastly, and most importantly, Paul was ready to communicate not only the Gospel but also himself (v. 8). It was all these aspects of his teaching that made his ministry among the Thessalonians so successful.

When Is Church Discipline Necessary?

Key Verses: 2 Thessalonians 3:6-13

I. Each Church Must Evaluate the Conduct of Her Members
   A. The Christians in Thessalonica were commanded in the name of the Lord by Paul to withdraw themselves from every brother who "walketh disorderly" (2 Thess. 3:6).
   B. The Lord Himself gave the apostles a mandate to discipline (Matt. 16:18, 19; John 20:22, 23) as representatives of the church (Matt. 18:18). Private offenses were first to be confessed to God (1 John 1:9) and then to each other (James 5:16). When rebuke and remonstrance failed, however (Matt. 18:15; cf. 1 Thess. 5:14), the wrongdoer was to be reprimanded in front of the whole church (Gal. 2:11; 1 Tim. 5:20). The elders of a local church may stand for representatives of a local church as it was organized in Jerusalem (Acts 15:6). If the accused person still remained obdurate in the case of blatant sin, the church proceeded to expulsion (Rom. 16:17; 1 Cor. 5:2, 11, 13; 2 John 1:10). In extreme cases, God Himself occasionally physically removed the person from this life (Acts 5:1–10; 8:24; 1 Cor. 5:5). The ultimate punishment was separation from Christ (Rom. 9:3; 1 Cor. 16:22; Gal. 1:8), which in reality would be impossible for those chosen by God (John 10:28).

When Is Church Discipline Necessary?

    C. The real aim of censure, however, was the future restoration of the erring member to fellowship (2 Cor. 2:5–10; Gal. 6:1; Jude 1:22, 23) as well as the prevention of sin's contamination in the church.

II. What Constitutes Disorderly Conduct?
    A. We would probably expect the sins listed in 1 Corinthians 5:11: fornication, idolatry, drunkenness and extortion.
    B. We may be surprised, on the other hand, to see Paul censure laziness and a refusal to work. These sins of omission are much misunderstood in our day of social welfare, and Paul's command, "if any would not work, neither should he eat" (2 Thess. 3:10) sounds harsh to modern ears.
    C. Furthermore, Christians must mind their own business and not be busybodies (2 Thess. 3:11). Even sensationalism about the coming of the Lord constitutes disorderly conduct (2 Thess. 2:2, 3).
    D. In addition to providing for ourselves, we should "not be weary in well doing" for those truly in need (2 Thess. 3:13).
    E. Paul would have considered himself walking in a disorderly manner had he become a financial burden to the local congregation or to other fellow believers (2 Thess. 3:8). What an example for the modern churchgoer who seeks to be served more than to serve!

For What and for Whom Should a Christian Pray?

Key Verses: 1 Timothy 2:1-8

I. What Is Prayer?
   A. Prayer is communion with God. Since God is spirit (John 4:24), we can communicate with Him only with our spirit.
   B. Only those human spirits will be heard which have responded to God's initiative. If man has not accepted God's initiative, he cannot pray in the sense of truly communicating with God (Ps. 66:18).
   C. Yet all who seek God can pray because all humans possess a spirit, the only means through which man can communicate with God.
   D. Paul prayed before he was saved, but there was a distinct character to his prayer after he was saved. The Lord said to Ananias about converted Saul: "Behold he prayeth." From the moment of the conversion Paul became truly a man of prayer.

II. Paul Was a Man of Prayer
   A. In prayer the Lord spoke to him (Acts 22:17–21).
   B. For him prayer was the realization of God's presence (Eph. 1:16–18; 1 Thess. 1:2, 3).
   C. He found that the Holy Spirit assisted him in prayer as he sought to know and do God's will (Rom. 8:14, 26).
   D. Prayer for Paul was a gift of the Spirit (1 Cor. 14:1–16). The believer prays in the Spirit (Eph. 6:18; Jude 1:20). Therefore, prayer for the believer is a cooperation be-

tween God and himself, in that it is presented to the Father, in the Name of the Son, through the inspiration of the indwelling Holy Spirit.

III. Prayer in the Name of Jesus
   A. Prayer is a new concept in the New Testament (John 16:24).
   B. It does not imply that prayer should be made to the Son instead of to the Father, but the idea is to pray in the Spirit, through the Son, to the Father.
   C. Therefore, only prayer "in the Name of Jesus" will be answered. But what is sought must coincide with what the character, purpose, and plan of Jesus Christ is for the whole world. The Father will not grant any prayer which will not make Christ recognizable for all that He is. Answered prayer is what God directs or permits, not necessarily in agreement with what we ask, but with what He deems necessary for Him to accomplish in and through us. He who obeys God's will is he who considers his prayers always answered.

IV. We Must Pray for Others
   A. We must pray for others because of the temptations they face.
   B. That "therefore" in 1 Timothy 2:1 is important and must connect with 1 Timothy 1:18–20, which speaks of Hymenaeus and Alexander who had made shipwreck insofar as the faith is concerned. The implication is that had believers who knew them prayed for them, they might not have suffered shipwreck. How many of our acquaintances would have been helped had we faithfully prayed for them!
   C. Others must take first place on our prayers. This is what is meant by "first of all."
   D. The Greek phrase *"prōton pántōn,"* first of all, can also mean that before everything else in our relation to others, we must pray.

E. We must pray not only for individuals even as Christ did for Peter (Luke 22:32), the soldiers at the cross (Luke 23:34), but also for all the saints (Eph. 6:18) and as Paul says, "for all men" (1 Tim. 2:1).

F. These include those who rule over us, kings and all in authority. Our prayer for these is that "we may lead a quiet and peaceable life in all godliness and honesty" and that they be saved.

V. **Prayer Takes Various Forms**

A. Actually, Paul's admonition is not just to pray, but that "supplications, prayers, intercessions, and giving of thanks be made for all men." What are all these? They are forms of prayer which detail its purpose and manner. Let us see what they mean:

1. "Supplications" is *deḗseis*, the plural of *déēsis*. It involves prayer for a particular need and this need must be perceived and discerned by the praying one through the Spirit within him. We are not requested by Paul to pray for people's desires or wants to be fulfilled, but for what we perceive the needs are for their lives as the Holy Spirit reveals these to us.

2. "Prayers" is *proseuchás*, accusative plural of *proseuchḗ*, which is the most frequent word expressing prayer exclusively to God. It is a derivative from the preposition *prós*, toward, and *euchḗ*, a vow or wish. It is addressing God on behalf of others and ourselves.

3. "Intercessions" is *enteúxeis*, the plural of *énteuxis*, which, however, in 1 Timothy 4:5 is translated "prayer." The verb is *entugchánō* from *en*, in, and *tugchánō*, to get, attain. It is to make intercession for or against anyone (Rom. 8:27, 34; 11:2; Heb. 7:25). The noun means "meeting God on behalf of," that is, intercession. It is to pray on behalf of those who do not have access to God, such as

For What and for Whom Should a Christian Pray?

some rulers of this world (1 Tim 2:2) and the unsaved (v. 4).

4. And "giving of thanks" *eucharistías*, the plural of *eucharistía*, thanksgiving. The basic word is *cháris*, grace, with the prefix *eu*, good. We are exhorted to give thanks for all people. That is not easy, especially if they are unbelievers and rulers who may be ungodly. This means that:

   a) In all people there is something for which we can thank God even if it is that they let us alone to live a quiet and peaceable life.

   b) No matter who rules over us, they would not be there if it were not God's permissiveness or directive will (Rom. 13:1–3).

VI. Aggressive Prayerful Concern

A. The preposition used in the Greek and translated "for" in 1 Timothy 2:1, 2 in the phrases "for all men" and "for all that are in authority" is *hupér*, which could be translated "on behalf of" indicating God's salvation or favor accruing to their advantage. The meaning of *hupér* is actually "over." It implies these people are helpless, lying down insofar as their relationship with God is concerned, and we stand over them to help them be what God wants them to be. There should be an aggressiveness in our supplications, prayers, intercessions, and thanksgivings.

B. In Ephesians 6:18 where a similar admonition is made for all the saints, the preposition is *perí*, which is concerning, in regard to, with a less aggressive initiative. And in Ephesians 6:19 where Paul refers to himself and his evangelistic effort, the preposition reverts to *hupér*.

C. Conclusion: There should be certain priorities in our seeking the face of God on behalf of others. Rulers over us, the salvation of sinners, and the efforts to evangelize them must have certain aggressive priority.

Paul's Thoughts Just Before His Death

Key Verses: 2 Timothy 1:1–14

I. Paul's Last Letter
   A. Paul was in prison in Rome waiting for his trial with the probable imminent verdict of death (2 Tim. 4:6–8).
   B. He wanted his son in the faith, Timothy, to hurry to him.
   C. Timothy was laboring in Asia Minor when he received this letter.

II. Paul Does Not Lament His Faith
   A. Not a word of complaint is uttered.
   B. He asserts that his apostleship was through the will of God (v. 1).
   C. He was facing death and yet he speaks about "the promise of life in Christ Jesus" (v. 1). It was the same apostle who wrote "for me to live is Christ and to die is gain" (Phil. 1:21).

III. Paul's Attitude Toward Timothy
   A. He calls him "beloved child" (v. 2). The word is not "son," *huiós*, which indicates maturity and independence. Paul never calls Timothy *huiós*, but always *téknon* (1 Tim. 1:2, 18; 2 Tim. 1:2; 2:1) an appellation of tenderness expressive of the time of his spiritual birth. The noun derives from *tíktō*, to give birth to. We should never forget our children in the faith no matter

where their spiritual growth is. At the hour of impending death, remembering how many spiritual children we have helped bring forth spells great comfort.
B. Paul remembered Timothy in his prayers (v. 3).
1. Unceasingly. The Greek word is *adiáleipton*, an adjective which means without intermission, unceasing remembering. This does not mean that Paul did nothing else but remember Timothy constantly, but rather that whatever Paul did, he did it in such a way that the recalling of it would affect and influence Timothy. The same adjective occurs also in Romans 9:2 only as Paul thought of the stubbornness of his fellow Jews in their rejection of Christ. ". . . I have great heaviness and continual (*adiáleipton*) sorrow in my heart." The word for sorrow is *odúnē*, which means birth pangs. Every time Paul thought of Israel he experienced pain because of their unbelief.
2. In a similar manner is Paul's exhortation in 1 Thessalonians 5:17, "Pray without ceasing" (the adverb *adialeíptōs*). Whatever we undertake to do, we must pray in its performance. It does not mean that we must pray to the exclusion of work; rather, we must saturate our work with prayer and the consciousness of how it would influence others.
C. Paul prayed for Timothy's particular, specific needs.
1. The word used is not *proseuchaí*, the general word for prayers, but *déēseis*, supplications, for particular needs of Timothy. That is how we should pray for those for whom we are concerned.
2. Paul must have spent sleepless nights to be able to pray not only during the day, but also at night. Prayer is the most wonderful engagement in the enjoyment of a sleepless night.

IV. Memory Is Sharpest at the Hour of Death

A. One of the greatest desires of man when dying is to see his loved ones for the last time on earth. Such was Paul's eager, earnest desire (v. 4).

B. What were Timothy's tears which Paul remembered? Those Timothy shed when the two parted as Paul left him to spend the winter in Nicopolis (Titus 3:12) in Epirus, Greece. Tears are an expression of love and concern, not necessarily weakness and desperation. Paul shed many tears at Ephesus (Acts 20:19, 31). The Ephesian elders wept as Paul was leaving them (Acts 20:37). Paul's concern for the Corinthians expressed itself by many tears (2 Cor. 2:4). The memory of tears is far stronger and more impressive in a man's last hours than the memory of joyous occasions. There is a blessing in tears (Luke 6:21).

V. The Memory of Genuine Faith (v. 5)

A. Paul calls Timothy's faith unfeigned, which in Greek is *anupokrítou*, without hypocrisy.

1. The faith that produces tears often spells genuineness. In 1 Timothy 1:2 he calls him a genuine child in the faith.

2. Timothy's faith was encouraged by his grandmother and mother, who may have believed before he did. If their faith had not been genuine, Timothy would probably never have followed Christ. These were Jewish believers whose study of the Old Testament prepared them for the acceptance of the Messiah through Paul's preaching in response to his ministry at Lystra, Timothy being a native of that place.

3. Noteworthy is the absence of his father, who was a Greek and a native of Lystra (Acts 16:1). In spite of the mixed marriage, the influence of a godly mother and grandmother prevailed. His father might have died by the time Paul got to Lystra.

4. We do not know for sure when Timothy became a Christian. The testimony of his mother and grandmother must have influenced him in the acceptance of the Gospel preached by Paul during his first missionary journey (2 Tim. 3:11). His heart must have been prepared by the prior acceptance of Christ by his mother and grandmother to receive Paul's message. Paul must have had a direct influence on Timothy since he repeatedly calls him his child in the faith (1 Tim. 1:2, 18; 2 Tim. 1:2; 2:1).

5. Timothy's faith, although influenced by his mother and grandmother, was not automatically transmitted but resulted from his own personal acceptance of Christ. Observe the last words of verse 5, "And I am persuaded that in thee also." The verb here is *pépeismai*, the perfect middle passive of *peíthō*, to persuade. The meaning is middle, "I have persuaded myself" that the unhypocritical, genuine faith that indwelt his mother and grandmother also indwelt him. The verb for "in thee dwelleth" is *enṓkēsen*, the aorist of *enoikéō*, to indwell, from the preposition *en*, in, and *oikéō*, to dwell as if in a house. The house was their hearts as well as his. This is the only place where we read of faith indwelling. We do have, however, the indwelling of the Holy Spirit in Christians (Rom. 8:11; 2 Tim. 1:14); the divine presence and blessing (1 Cor. 3:16; 2 Cor. 6:16, dwells in—*oikeí en*); the indwelling of the word of Christ (Col. 3:16). Christ's faith is never inherited, but one's decision is influenced by a godly family. Christ's faith must be personally accepted.

Preaching That Soothes The Audience

Key Verses: 2 Timothy 3:14; 4:5

I. **In the Last Days People Will Depart from the Truth**
   A. Paul begins in 2 Timothy 4:3, "For the time will come." The word for time is *kairós*, season. The moral and spiritual situation in society will be such that the people will not tolerate an unchangeable, fixed gospel. Instead, they will adhere to relative truth and situational ethics. They will want to hear what conforms to the times.
   B. People will progressively deteriorate as Paul warns Timothy in 2 Timothy 3:1: "This know also, that in the last days perilous times [*kairoí*] shall come." The word for "perilous" is *chalepoí*, which means fierce. This is the word used in the Greek classics to typify dogs and wild swine (e.g., *Xenophōntos Anábasis* 5, 8, 24). Likewise, it is used to describe the demoniacs in Matthew 8:28.
   C. Jeremiah lamented in his day that the religious leaders were conforming to the low morality of the people: "The prophets prophesy falsely, and the priests bear rule by their means; and my people love to have it so: and what will ye do in the end thereof?" (Jer. 5:31). The prophets and priests were those whose task it was to convey God's message as eternal and unchangeable. In an evil age, however, it was easier to please the people by perverting God's truth rather than by proclaiming it.

II. God's Truth Cannot Be Changed
  A. When God's Word convicts us, we must change ourselves and not the truth. The consequences of our disobedience cannot be altered no matter how much we distort the truth, as evidenced by the fall of Adam and Eve in the Garden of Eden.
  B. One example of changing truth to falsehood in our day involves the sanctity of life. Because man wants to be unrestrained in his use of God's sacred gift of sex, even the Supreme Court has declared abortion legal. The killing of a child out of the womb is considered murder, but not while it is still in the womb. Man has changed the rules to fit the times, "and the priests bear rule by their means" (Jer. 5:31). Although our government may make abortion legal, however, it cannot make it right.
  C. In reality, we cannot escape the consequences of this evil. Besides the tremendous loss of life, it has caused all of our lives to be devalued.

III. There Is a Dichotomy Between Man's Acceptance of the Physical and the Spiritual Laws of God
  A. When man discovers God's physical laws, he cannot but bow before them in perfect obedience. For instance, no one considers the law of gravity invalid because it is absolute. Indeed, if man wants to rise up instead of fall down, he must apply a force that counteracts gravity. He can never merely disregard it. In the spiritual realm, however, he deceives himself into thinking that he can bypass God's law because the consequences are not so readily apparent.
  B. Even though Adam and Eve did not die physically immediately after they had eaten the fruit of the tree of the knowledge of good and evil, nevertheless they instantly activated the aging process which eventually led to their death. They also abruptly severed their

communion with God as they sinned, which was the most disastrous consequence of all.

IV. Because of This Delusion, Man Desires Teachers Who Will Make Him Feel Good Rather Than Reveal the Truth
   A. Depraved man does not desire to hear that he is a sinner and that judgment awaits him (Heb. 9:27).
   B. Even the Christian often chooses material things first and the kingdom second. Consequently, he does not want teachers who remind him that his present life will indeed determine his future status in heaven (1 Cor. 3:11–15). Instead, he searches out preachers who will scratch his ears with their soothing messages.

Philemon and a Returned Wayward Slave, Onesimus

Key Verses: Philemon 1:1-12

I. Introduction
   A. Philemon was an influential Christian at Colossae.
   B. Onesimus was a runaway slave belonging to Philemon.
      1. He made the acquaintance of Paul in prison (Col. 4:9; Phile. 1:9, 10) and became a Christian. This took place either in Rome, during Paul's imprisonment (A.D. 62), or in Ephesus about A.D. 55.
      2. Either Rome or Ephesus might have attracted Onesimus by providing opportunity to hide among the great population.
      3. Onesimus had robbed his master, Philemon, and run away.
      4. There is the possibility that Onesimus was a brother in the flesh to Philemon (Phile. 1:16) or a compatriot.
         a) In the pagan world where slavery was prevalent, it was common to be born in slavery or as a child to be sold as a slave by one's parents. It was also possible to become a slave because one was unbearably poor. Debtors sometimes became slaves. Those captured in war or piracy or by kidnapping could also become slaves.
         b) Most probably Onesimus was Philemon's "brother in the flesh" who, because he was a derelict, was sold into slavery.

c) He had fled from the state of slavery and in this circumstance is found in Rome, 1,000 miles away.

C. How did Onesimus get in touch with Paul in prison in Rome?
1. He must have heard of Paul's connection with Colossae, his hometown, and with Philemon, his master.
2. He contacted Paul, which gave Paul opportunity to lead Onesimus to Christ. Paul spoke of having spiritually begotten Onesimus in his bonds (v. 10).

D. Onesimus, as a believer, stayed and served Paul in prison (v. 13).

II. Paul's Letter to the Colossians

A. Tychicus, an Asian, had accompanied Paul to Jerusalem as a delegate of his church with the collection (Acts 20:4; cf. 1 Cor. 16:1–4). Now in Rome with Paul, he is used by Paul to carry personally his letters to the Colossians (Col. 4:7–9) and Ephesians (Eph. 6:21, 22).

B. At that time when Tychicus was to take Paul's letter to the Colossians, Paul decided to send Onesimus back to Colossae and to Philemon.
1. Paul must have been sure of the genuineness of Onesimus' conversion.
2. He decided to test Philemon by giving him an opportunity to act toward his returned slave no longer in the relationship of master to slave, but of brother to brother.
3. Paul considered this as a unique opportunity to prove what Christ can do in restoring broken relationships.

III. The Social Implications of the Gospel

A. Onesimus had to be persuaded to return to Philemon, who could greatly punish his returned slave. The work

of Christ in an individual's life is only half accomplished if it stops with oneself. Every effort must be made to restore former relationships.
1. The big questions with Onesimus were:
   a) Will my master accept me? Paul may have told him the parable of the prodigal son returning to a home where he was viewed with suspicion and rejection by an older brother.
   b) Onesimus had to be persuaded by Paul and Epaphras, the founder of the churches in Colossae, Hierapolis (Col. 4:13), and Laodicea that his master was a fellow believer. See also Colossians 1:7; 4:12; Philemon 1:23. Epaphras had come to Paul in prison in Rome to inform him of the spiritual condition of the churches of the Lycus Valley, which moved Paul to write the Epistle to the Colossians. It was then that Paul may have discussed Onesimus' conversion with Epaphras.
   c) It was a great act of faith for Onesimus to risk everything by allowing the love of Christ to restore him to Philemon.
2. Paul, having persuaded Onesimus to go back to Philemon in Colossae, now has to persuade Philemon of Onesimus' faith by writing him this letter, which is truly a masterpiece.

IV. Paul's Persuasive Arguments
   A. He appeals to his present condition of imprisonment (v. 1).
   B. He conjoins Timothy's entreaty (v. 1).
   C. He appeals not only to Philemon, but also to Apphia, probably his wife, and one Archippus, a spiritual fellow soldier of Paul and Timothy. This is as if Paul were asking Philemon to consult others there in considering Paul's request for Onesimus, who undoubtedly was well-known to them all.

D. Paul wanted Philemon not to consider this merely as a personal matter but as it would affect "the church in thy house" (v. 2).
E. Paul speaks of the love and faith of Philemon (vv. 4, 5).
F. He gently reminds Philemon that the faith he experienced is a common faith (the fellowship, *koinōnía*, from *koinós*, common) which must be energized in extending the good effect (*agathón*, communicable good; v. 6).
G. He refers to Philemon's past benevolence (v. 7).
H. Paul does not command, but requests Philemon to do that which he needs to do toward Onesimus, not because of duty and apostolic authority, but because of love. What one does because of obligation never brings the same joy as when it is done from the love of Christ in his heart (vv. 8, 9, 14).
I. God's grace made Onesimus his son in the faith (v. 10).
J. God's grace made Onesimus, who was useless to Philemon, now useful both to him and to Paul. A useless derelict can be changed (vv. 11, 12).
K. Paul preferred to send Onesimus back to his master instead of enjoying the service he could render to him in prison (vv. 13, 15).
L. Paul promises personal restoration of anything Onesimus may have stolen from Philemon (v. 18). That which Onesimus could not do, Paul was willing to do on his behalf. This points out the importance of restoration (Luke 19:8) and sacrifice in order to restore another believer's honor.

Faith as a Conductor of Invaluable Knowledge

Key Verses: Hebrews 11:1-3, 8-19

I. Faith Enriches
   A. Although Abraham was at first compelled to dwell in tents, eventually his new land became a rich nation (Heb. 11:9).
   B. Sarah, unable to have children in her youth, bore Isaac when she was past the natural age according to God's promise (Heb. 11:11). Thus, Abraham became father of a numerous people.
   C. Likewise, all those who call upon the Lord become rich in knowledge (Rom. 10:12): "That in every thing ye are enriched by Him [Christ], in all utterance, and in all knowledge" (1 Cor. 1:5).

II. Faith Explains the Unexplainable
   A. "Through faith we understand that the worlds were framed by the word of God" (Heb. 11:3). The word for understanding used here is *noéō*, to apprehend by using one's mind. Unless we acknowledge God, it is impossible to ascertain just how the worlds did come into being. Any other explanation is only an improvised theory.
   B. Unbelievers, however, will not accept that "in the beginning God created heaven and the earth" (Gen. 1:1). The mere simplicity of this statement confounds the intellectual. Paul describes this paradox in 1 Corinthians 1:20, "Hath not God made foolish the wisdom of this world?" In other words, true wisdom must

begin with faith in God: "The fear of the Lord is the beginning of knowledge" (Prov. 1:7).

III. Faith Is Logical
   A. God exists.
   B. God is omnipotent and, therefore, can do anything He wills, including forming this world.
   C. Because He did not give humans a mind equal to His own, we are incapable of understanding His creative process. If God had given us such minds we would have been elevated to His level and would then not have honored Him as creator (Rom. 1:21). God would rather be worshiped by us than to be simply understood intellectually.
   D. However, in His great wisdom, He did give us a means whereby we could come to know and praise Him. That medium is faith.
   E. Our faith rests on Christ. Hebrews 11:1 states, "Now faith is the substance of things hoped for." The word for substance is *hupóstasis*, substantial or firm. We can trust Christ completely because of the indisputable fact of His resurrection (1 Cor. 15:4–8, 14, 17, 18). Thus, our faith is built upon facts and not fairy tales.

IV. What Is the Exclusive Knowledge of the Believer?
   A. The believer knows that Christ is God in the flesh (John 1:1, 14). Even more noteworthy is 1 John 5:20: "And we know [*oídamen*, intuitive knowledge which comes through faith] that the Son of God is come, and has given us an understanding, [*diánoian*, thorough understanding] that we may know [*ginōskomen*, experiential knowledge] him, that is true. . . ." In other words, we can actually come to know God in a personal way.

B. We know that we are saved and have become a new creation (John 3:16; 2 Cor. 5:17). In fact, we are now fit to call God, "Father" (Rom. 8:15).
C. This world, including ourselves, however, still labors under the effects of the curse of sin (Rom. 8:22).
D. Therefore, our hope is in a better world to come (Rom. 8:23; Rev. 21:1).
E. We have an explanation for the vicissitudes of life and realize that each event will turn out for good if we love and trust in God (Rom. 8:28).
F. No matter what occurs in this life, we know our eternal destiny is glorious (John 10:28; Rom. 8:38, 39; 2 Cor. 5:1; 1 John 3:2).
G. Until that time, however, we have access to God through prayer (1 John 5:14, 15).

V. **Unbelief Is Ignorance**
   A. Since faith is the medium for understanding the mysteries of this life, the unbelievers possess appalling and pitiable ignorance (Deut. 29:29; 1 Cor. 2:9–12).
   B. Furthermore, it is impossible to please God without having faith in Him. Thereby, the unbeliever forfeits all of the precious promises awarded by God to the faithful (Heb. 11:6).

Cure for Christian Weariness

Key Verses: Hebrews 12:1, 2, 12-17

I. The Christian Life Is a Struggle
   A. Although it is described as a race in Hebrews 12:1, it is not a competitive one. This misunderstanding comes from the word *agōn*, translated "race." It actually means struggle. The metaphor of the race, however, does depict that this struggle has a beginning and an end. The idea of surpassing other Christians, however, is not implied in the word.
   B. Rather, this is an individual race in which God has set a goal for each one of us. It is His desire that we each reach our goal.

II. In the Struggle, We Become Weary
   A. One important cause is physical exhaustion (Is. 40:31; 2 Cor. 4:16; Heb. 12:12). Due to sin, our physical body is in a state of decay and on a downhill course (Rom. 8:23).
   B. Secondly, we become wearied by external persecutions (Heb. 10:32-34). These, however, are to be considered a natural part of the Christian's experience on earth (John 15:18-21; 2 Tim. 3:10-12; 1 Pet. 4:12-16).
   C. Thirdly, we suffer from spiritual fatigue as we battle sin within as well as without (Heb. 12:1, 15). Paul describes the intensity of this struggle in Romans 7 and encourages us not "to lose heart in doing good" (Gal. 6:9). "Hands which hang down, and the feeble knees" (Heb. 12:12) convey such weariness.

III. God Gives Solutions
  A. We are admonished to "lift up the hands which hang down" (Heb. 12:12). The Greek word is *anorthōsate*, from *aná*, again, or *ánō*, up, and *orthóō*, to straighten or strengthen. The verb is in the active voice, indicating that it is within our power to act. In the case of physical exhaustion, we may need to rest and eat, as did Elijah when fleeing from Jezebel (1 Kgs. 19:4). When beset by illness, we may have to trust in God's grace, as Paul.
  B. External difficulties are to be faced with thanksgiving and joy (Phil. 3:1, 8; 4:6; James 1:2). We are to also seek peace with all men and be careful not to let a root of bitterness spring up because of persecution (Heb. 12:14, 15). Jesus gives even more practical advice as to how this attitude is to be achieved (Matt. 5:44).
  C. Finally, in battling internal sin, we are admonished to "lay aside every weight, and the sin which doth so easily beset us," while considering Jesus and all the faithful before us (Heb. 12:1).

Two Mountains Contrasted

Key Verses: Hebrews 12:18-29

I. At the End of Hebrews 12, Two Mountains Are Compared
   A. Mt. Sinai (Heb. 12:18) where God delivered the Commandments to Moses, is contrasted with Mt. Zion (v. 22), where the believers of all ages will assemble.
   B. Mt. Sinai is synonymous with the Law, which caused fear; while Mt. Zion is synonymous with grace, which brought fulfillment.

II. Mt. Sinai and Its Accomplishments
   A. It burned with fire and was surrounded by blackness (Heb. 12:18).
   B. A severe storm also enveloped it (Heb. 12:18).
   C. A trumpet preceded pronouncements so difficult that the people begged that no more be given (Heb. 12:19).
   D. Even an animal must die if it so much as touched the mountain (Heb. 12:20).
   E. Moses, a man of great faith, was filled with fear at the sight of it (Heb. 12:21).

III. Mt. Sinai (the Law) Was Not God's Goal for Man
   A. For this reason, verse 18 begins with a negative. "For ye are not come unto the mount [Sinai]. . . ."
   B. The Law brought condemnation, not salvation (Rom. 3:20; 4:15; Gal. 3:13).
   C. It was merely a stepping stone described as, "our schoolmaster to bring us into Christ" (Gal. 3:24).

IV. God's Real Desire for His People Is Mt. Zion (Grace)
   A. Mt. Zion, the highest mountain in Jerusalem, represents a heavenly place.
   B. It does not depict the earthly Church, for that is only the pathway to the heavenly Jerusalem, which is our ultimate destination (Heb. 11:10, 16; 13:14; Rev. 21:2, 10).
   C. While in the general assembly on earth in the Church, we have tribulation (John 16:33), in heaven we will participate in a festal gathering or *panēguris*, "general assembly" (Heb. 12:23).
      1. Only those whose names are written in the book of life will be on Mt. Zion in the heavenly Jerusalem (Phil. 4:3; Heb. 12:23; Rev. 3:5; 13:8; 17:8; 20:12, 15).
      2. There the church will be judged to receive rewards (Rom. 14:10; 2 Cor. 5:10). The first born or *prōtotókōn* (Heb. 12:23), are those who will be ranked first.
      3. All the spirits of the righteous will be made perfect there (Heb. 12:23), and they shall dwell with God forever (Rev. 21:3).

V. Jesus Christ Determines the Difference (Heb. 12:24)
   A. A residence on Mt. Zion is assured by the mediator or guarantor, Jesus Christ, when we put our faith in Him (Acts 16:31).
   B. The mountain represents the new covenant of grace which He mediates.
   C. This transition is made possible only through the shed blood of Jesus Christ (Heb. 9:14, 22; 1 John 1:7).

Principles of Christian Conduct

Key Verses: Hebrews 13:1-5

I. **Brotherly Love Must Abide (Heb. 13:1)**
   A. Love of the brethren is the mark of a Christian (John 17:21, 23; 1 John 2:9–11; 3:10, 16, 17; 4:20, 21).
   B. This love is to continue no matter what the circumstances.

II. **Hospitality Is Not to Be Forgotten (Heb. 13:2)**
   A. We are commanded to make strangers welcome in our home (Rom. 12:13; 1 Tim. 3:2; Titus 1:8; 1 Pet. 4:9).
   B. Strangers may even turn out to be angels Heb. 13:2; cf. Gen. 18:3; 19:2).

III. **Remember Those Who Are in Prison for the Sake of the Gospel (v. 3)**
   A. Paul calls himself such a prisoner, *désmios* (Acts 23:18; 28:17; Eph. 3:1; 4:1; 2 Tim. 1:8).
   B. As members of the body of Christ, when one is bound physically or spiritually, all of us must consider ourselves bound with him (1 Cor 12:26).

IV. **Remember Also Those Who Are Afflicted in Other Ways (v. 3)**
   A. Another translation for the Greek word *kakouchéō* (suffer adversity) is "to have it bad." We are not to disdain such brethren but help them (Gal. 6:2).
   B. Listed in the gallery of faith in Hebrews 11:37 are those said to have been *kakouchoúmenoi*, tormented

(KJV); ill-treated (NASB); mistreated (NIV). Indeed, it is an honor to suffer for the name of Christ (Acts 5:41).

V. **Marriage Is to Be Upheld in Honor (v. 4)**
   A. The word translated "honorable" is *tímios*, from *timḗ*, which means honor or esteem. Marriage vows are not to be taken lightly but rather to be considered a lifelong commitment.
   B. Marriage brings value to all aspects of life. Unfortunately, the two Greek words *en pásin*, translated "in all" (KJV); "among all" (NASB); and by all (NIV); do not fully convey the exegetical meaning. Marriage should be respected by all, but it also adds value to all of life. In 1 Corinthians 7:26–35, Paul describes his desire to stay single due to the hardships of his itinerant ministry. His high regard for the marriage commitment is thus demonstrated.

VI. **Sex Must Be Within Marriage**
   A. The KJV has the word *koítē*, translated as bed, while the NASB and the NIV have it designated as the marriage bed. It simply means a bed that is shared (Luke 11:7; Rom. 13:13). There is a positive statement here that sex within marriage is good and necessary (1 Cor. 7:3–5).
   B. But sex outside marriage is totally condemned.
      1. Whoremongers is *pórnoi*, those engaging in all kinds of extra-marital sexual immorality.
      2. Adulterers is *moichoí*, involving a married spouse.
      3. Such people will be judged as described in Revelation 21:8 and 22:15.

VII. **Contentment (v. 5)**
   A. "Conversation" here is *trópos*, or way of life, daily behavior.

B. "Without covetousness" is *aphilárguros,* in the Greek, without love of silver or money.
C. The believer rather is to set his affection on things above, not on the things of the earth (Col. 3:2). In this way, we will be content with any circumstances we experience here.

The Hope Born of the Resurrection of Christ

Key Verses: 1 Peter 1:3-9

I. **God Is Inherently Trustworthy, Blessed, and Praiseworthy**
   A. The word with which 1 Peter 1:3 begins is "blessed." This is not the Beatitude word *makários,* which is the quality of deity (1 Tim. 1:11; when man becomes *makários,* "blessed," because of Jesus Christ [Matt. 5:11] he is indwelt by God, and becomes fully satisfied.) The word used in 1 Peter 1:3 and Ephesians 1:3, however, is an entirely different word, *eulogētós,* from the verb *eulogéō,* "to speak well of." The adjective *eulogētós,* "blessed," is ascribed only to God (Mark 14:61; Luke 1:68; Rom. 1:25; 9:5; 2 Cor. 1:3; 11:31; Eph. 1:3; 1 Pet. 1:3) who is inherently worthy of our praise. When the Virgin Mary is spoken of as "blessed," (Luke 1:28, 42) the adjective used is *eulogēménē,* the perfect passive participle of *eulogéō* meaning one made blessed or praiseworthy by God and not on her own.
   B. No matter how God deals with us, He is praiseworthy. Apart from what He does for us, we should praise Him simply because He is God. Paul tells us in Philippians 3:1 to "rejoice in the Lord" no matter what our circumstances.

II. **God Is Also to Be Praised for What He Did for Us: Mercy, Regeneration, and Grace**
   A. First of all, He showed mercy to us. "Which [who] according to his abundant mercy. . . ." Mercy is *éleos,*

which means "pity for the consequences of our sin." Peter further states that He showed much pity. The abundance of His mercy is demonstrated by the sending of His own Son (John 3:16; Rom. 5:8).

B. Because of His pity, God regenerated us. The KJV says, "hath begotten us again" (1 Pet. 1:3). The Greek word is *anagennḗsas*, the aorist active participle of *anagennáō*, "to give new birth to," or "regenerate." This verb occurs only in 1 Peter 1:3, 23. In other words, God took the initiative to give us new birth.

C. He did not pity us in word only but also in action (as we are also advised to do in the Book of James, not only to pity others but to be benevolent toward them). The word in Greek which incorporates both pity and action is *cháris*, "grace," and the verb is *charitóō* (see Luke 1:28 and Eph. 1:6). When God extends His grace to us, He actually causes a change in us or gives us "new birth," *anagénnēsis*.

III. **God Gives Living Hope as Our Inheritance: Confidence, and Incorruptibility**

A. The salvation wrought by Christ on the cross creates hope in the believer (Rom. 8:24) while he who has no God has no hope (Eph. 2:12). This confidence in God can be "a very present help in trouble" as expressed in Ps. 46:1.

B. The fact that Jesus rose from the dead makes our hope a living one because we know that we too shall rise (Col. 1:18; 1 Pet. 1:3). Such an inheritance is "incorruptible," *áphthartos* (1 Pet. 1:4). It cannot degenerate no matter how difficult or corrupting the circumstances of this life are (1 Cor. 9:25; 15:52; 1 Pet. 1:23). The hope of our resurrection "fadeth not away," (a complementary word), *amárantos* which is used only in 1 Peter 1:4. The reason for its endurance is that it is kept for us in heaven where it is incorruptible. Not only do we experience external life here, but we shall experience it in its fullness in heaven (Rom. 8:23; 1 Cor. 15:52–54). At such time our regeneration, which began as we placed our trust in Christ (Eph. 1:13, 14), will be made complete (1 Pet. 1:9). Our present affliction is only temporary and will be amply repaid when we receive our heavenly inheritance of eternal life (1 Pet. 1:6, 7). This is the hope born of the resurrection of Christ and kept by our faith in Him (1 Pet. 1:5).

Desire Health Food, Discard Junk Food, and Grow Up

Key Verses: 1 Peter 2:2-10

I. Desire the Pure Growth Ingredient (v. 2)
   A. The verb "desire" is given as a command and in Greek is *epipothḗsate*, the aorist direct imperative of *epipothéō*. It means to desire earnestly, to long for (Rom. 1:11; 2 Cor. 5:2; 9:14; Phil. 1:8; 2:26; 1 Thess. 3:6; 2 Tim. 1:4). *Epipothéō* denotes not only earnestly desiring in the heart but also a willingness to do everything possible to achieve one's longed for ends. That the aorist tense (*epipothḗsate*) is used instead of the present imperative (*epipotheíte*) also indicates that such desire is active regarding its goal and objective, not merely passive and subjective. Just as with food, there should be a repetitive desire for spiritual wisdom for each individual choice that has to be made. It is a process of acquiring, digesting, and then desiring again.
   B. To continue the analogy of food, what is it that we are to so earnestly desire to eat? The KJV says, "desire the sincere milk of the word." The NASB says, "long for the pure milk of the word." The NIV has it, "crave pure spiritual milk." The Greek says "*tó logikón ádolon gála epipothḗsate*," the logical, unadulterated milk, greatly desire (and get). Note that the Greek verse does not have "of the word" as do both the KJV and NASB; the NIV has translated it closest to the original Greek, "crave pure, **spiritual** [*logikón*] milk."

1. The adjective *logikós* derives from *lógos*, "intelligence," or "someone or something immaterial." (In John 1:1 Christ is described in this way [*ho lógos*] before His incarnation.) *Logikós* also occurs in Romans 12:1 and refers to *latreía*, "serving as one worships in public." In other words, our service in public worship must have beyond its material aspect a spiritual significance. The only other place *logikós* occurs is here in 1 Peter 2:2 and must, therefore, be translated as "spiritual milk." As one needs material milk for his physical growth, so also he requires spiritual food for his spiritual growth.
2. The milk in 1 Peter 2:2 is also described as "sincere" (KJV); "pure" (NASB and NIV). The mistake of the translators in this case is that they have made a negative adjective into a positive one. "Sincere" in Greek is *eilikrinḗs*, and "pure" is *katharós*. *Ádolos*, on the other hand, derives from the privative alpha (*a–*), "without," and *dólos*, "deceit, fraud, guile." The word really comes from *délear*, "bait." When one baits a trap, he presents something deceptively good. *Ádolos*, which is the word used, must therefore be rendered as a negative adjective, "without deceit." But how can one beguile people when it comes to milk? Such fraud occurs when someone mixes another substance with it, such as water. *Ádolos*, therefore, in its relation to milk in this metaphor must be translated "unadulterated, unmixed." The warning over the possibility of mixing untruth with truth is evident in this passage. If one drinks milk mixed with water, he will be deficient in his nourishment. Unfortunately, many Christians drink adulterated spiritual milk. No wonder they suffer from spiritual anemia!

Desire Health Food, Discard Junk Food, and Grow Up

II. **Distinguish the Evil Growth Inhibitors**
   A. Before earnestly desiring unadulterated spiritual milk, we must eliminate the junk food that steals our appetites.
   B. First Peter 2:1 begins with the participle *apothémenoi*, "laying aside," which is the aorist participle middle of *apotíthēmi*, derived from *apó*, "from" (implying from oneself), and *títhēmi*, "to lay or set or put." Thus the correct translation of the first few words in this passage is "having put away from you" or "since, therefore, you did put away from you." (The verb *apotíthēmi* also occurs in Matt. 14:3; Acts 7:58; Rom. 13:12; Eph. 4:22, 25; Col. 3:8; Heb. 12:1; James 1:21).
   C. The putting off of certain bad habits and attitudes from the old life is absolutely necessary for a newly-born spiritual baby before he can develop a craving for true, unadulterated spiritual food. Our appetites for such are often lost because we carry into our Christian lives such putrefaction as Peter lists in verse 1. These are inhibitors of good spiritual taste.
      1. First mentioned is *kakía*, "unexternalized bad feelings, constitutional malice." Peter here indicates that there is a variety of such malice and that every kind of it ought to be discarded.
      2. "All guile" in Greek is *pánta dólon* (the same word as in *ádolon* of v. 2). Again, Peter says to get rid of every kind of guile.
      3. Next he mentions hypocrisies or *hupokríseis*, which means pretentions.
      4. "Envies," *phthónous*, "wishing evil on others for personal gain" is another aspect of our lives which must be removed.
      5. Lastly, Peter lists "and all evil speakings," *pásas katalaliás*, "speaking out false gossip or slander." Having heard something bad about somebody is

no reason to repeat it to anyone else. Thus, when a Christian finds his spiritual appetite for God's truth dulled, he should search for some of these clinging sins as detailed in 1 Peter 2:1 and also in Galatians 5:19–21; Ephesians 4:31; and Colossians 3:8.

God's Word and the Splitting of the Atom

Key Verses: 2 Peter 3:8-14

I. The Splitting of the Atom Was Foretold in the Bible
   A. Over 1,900 years ago the Word of God prophesied that the atom would be split. In 2 Peter 3:10 we read, "... the elements shall melt with fervent heat." The Greek word for "elements" is *stoicheía*, the physical elements or constituents of the universe.
   B. This reference was made in connection with "the day of the Lord" (v. 10); "the last days" (v. 3); and "His coming," *parousía* (v. 4).
      1. At this time, the second great catastrophe of the earth is to occur by fire (vv. 7, 12), the first being by water in the Noachic flood (Gen. 6:9-17; 2 Pet. 3:5, 6).
      2. This lurid picture of the final destruction will only affect ungodly people (v. 7), or "scoffers" (v. 3); however, just as in previous calamities, the ungodly perished while righteous Noah and Lot were saved (Gen. 6:9—7:10; 2 Pet. 2:5, 6). At the end time the believers will look beyond the destruction of the earth to "new heavens and a new earth, wherein dwelleth righteousness" (v. 13). In fact, certain passages in the Bible indicate some will avoid physical death altogether (1 Thess. 1:10; 4:17).

II. Peter Was Centuries Ahead of His Time
   A. In the Fifth Century B.C., the Greek philosophers Leucippus and Democritus first introduced the theory

that the basic unit of matter was an atom. The Greek word consists of the prefix *a–*, "without" and the verb *témnō*, "to divide." It was thus thought that the atom was unable to be split. Because of their postulation of this theory, the institute of atomic research in Athens today is called "Democritus."

B. One of the last Greek philosophers, Philo of Alexandria, whose fame reached a pinnacle in 25–50 A.D. just a few years prior to the writing of 2 Peter, referred to the elements of the universe as earth, water, air and fire. And yet, Peter did not follow this false theory in his letter but spoke of the elements, without numbering them: "the elements shall melt with fervent heat. . . ." This lack of reference to current thinking on the subject is a further indication that the Scriptures are not the product of human ingenuity but of divine inspiration (1 Cor. 2:7–16; 2 Tim. 3:16).

III. Despite Greek Ideas to the Contrary, the Splitting of the Atom Became a Reality in Our Century

A. The Word of God proved to be true. The doubt that some have expressed about the canonicity of 2 Peter should be dispelled on the basis of his significant prophecy about the splitting of the elements. If scientists were also students of God's Word, maybe the splitting of the atom would not have taken almost two thousand years.

IV. Peter Is Completely Accurate in His Terminology in View of Modern Thinking

A. He does not use the definite article with "elements" which would have possibly indicated that all atoms were to be split. In fact, only selected ones have so far been divided, such as uranium and plutonium.

B. The Greek word for "shall melt" is *luthēsontai*, the future indicative of *lúō*, basically meaning "to separate the constituent parts of which a unit consists." This choice of verb then perfectly describes the splitting of the atom. The opposite verb, *sunístēmi*, "hold together," is used in Colossians 1:17, ". . . and by him all things consist." Just as Jesus Christ now holds the atoms together, it is He who is going to bring about the end of the universe as we know it by splitting up that which He had previously assembled (Col. 1:16). What man has been able to accomplish with much effort, God will do with the ease of a simple word.

C. Peter also mentions in 2 Peter 3:10 that this splitting will be performed ". . . with fervent heat" an observation characteristic of atomic energy.

D. ". . . the heavens shall pass away with a great noise." The expression "with a great noise" in Greek is *rhoizēdón*. The onomatopoeia of the Greek word imitates the sound of the wind. In like manner, the noise accompanying the explosion of an atomic bomb is the deafening crash of air.

E. Peter ends verse 10 with the Greek word *kausoúmena*, the present participle of *kausóomai*, or *kausoúmai*, used only in the passive and meaning "being set on fire, burning." The word is used only in 2 Peter 3:10, 12. As the elements are burning, some shall be dissolved or split, and the earth and everything in it shall be totally destroyed.

V. This Important Prophecy Concerning the Destruction of the Earth by Fire Is Amply Documented in the Rest of Scripture

References to it are found in Psalms 50:3; 97:5; Isaiah 66:15, 16; Ezekiel 20:47, 48; Joel 2:30; Zephaniah 1:18; 3:8; and Malachi 4:1.

The Eternal God

Key Verses: Revelation 1:4-8

I. God Is Designated as the Same in the Past, Present, and Future: "Which Is and Which Was, and Which Is to Come . . ." (Rev. 1:4)
   A. One edition of the Greek New Testament, the Majority Text, says, "Grace unto you and peace from God, who is and who was and which is to come." However, the expression *apó Theoú*, from God, is missing from some other texts. Exegetically, the Majority Text is the most acceptable. Indeed, the grace (*cháris*) that transforms a human being (Eph. 2:8) and the peace that reconciles man to God (Rom. 5:1) can only come from God. The fact that the definite article is missing before God indicates the Triune God, as opposed to any particular personality in the Trinity.
   B. The three tenses of the verb which follow "from God" show that God is without time limitations.
   C. Although we are creatures of time, God as its creator cannot be limited by time.

II. A More Accurate Translation Strengthens the Sense of God's Infinity
   A. In the Greek text the first verb is really a participial noun. Therefore, it should be translated "who being" instead of "who is." It means the ever present one, *ho ōn*.
   B. John then writes, "*kaí ho ēn*," the one who had been. The word *ēn* is the imperfect of the Greek verb *eimí*, to be. It is in the indicative mood because there is no participial form indicating the timeless past. As far as the past is concerned, God had always been.

C. What is translated "and which is to come" in Greek is *kaí ho erchómenos*, literally meaning "and the one who will keep coming." This verb is not in the indicative future referring to a once-and-for-all coming, but rather, describes God's eternal existence in the future.

III. **That Which Is Spoken of God Is Also True of Christ**
   A. "And from Jesus Christ . . ." (Rev. 1:5). It is to Jesus that the words of Revelation 1:5–7 are referring.
   B. Similarly, in Revelation 1:10, Jesus is called "Alpha and Omega," the first and last letters of the Greek alphabet. This metaphor is another way of showing Jesus' eternity as part of the Triune God.

IV. **God Is an Ever-Present Help**
   A. God will help us live in the present despite our circumstances.
   B. Because of Jesus' momentous sacrifice, all our past sins are washed away when we believe in Him.
   C. Furthermore, we can have hope in the future because of His trustworthy promises.

The State of Christian Believers

Key Verses: Revelation 21:1-6

I. The Believer's Present State Is Incomplete
   A. While Christ redeemed our souls and spirits, He has not yet redeemed our bodies (Rom. 8:23).
   B. We now have only the firstfruits of the Spirit (Rom. 8:23). *Aparchē*, the first fruit, is something given at the beginning of a process with much more to follow. It is the same word used in 1 Corinthians 15:20, 23, referring to Christ's resurrection and guaranteeing ours in the future

II. Our Present State Is Burdensome
   A. Tears, pain, and suffering are inevitable accompaniments of mortal life, which will someday disappear (Rev. 21:4).
   B. While Christ paid the penalty for our total redemption on the cross (Is. 53:4; Matt. 8:17; Acts 4:10, 12; 1 Pet. 2:24), yet only part of it is realized here and now. The perfection of our body will not be accomplished until the environment is also changed (Rom. 8:21, 22; Rev. 21:1).

III. The Tribulation Will Be a Time of Accentuated Trouble
   A. All believers, dead and alive, will be spared the calamity (1 Thess. 4:13–17).
   B. During this period the Gospel will be preached and new converts made from among both Jews and Gentiles (Rev. 7:1–9).
   C. These believers will endure the worst tribulation period the world has ever known (Matt. 24:21, 22; Rev. 7:14).

D. It is in this context that "God shall wipe away all tears from their eyes" (Rev. 7:17).

IV. **At Last, All Believers Will Receive an Incorruptible Body**
   A. This final state comes about as God creates a qualitatively new (*kainós*) heaven and earth (Rev. 21:1).
   B. Simultaneously, our former corruptible and mortal bodies shall be clothed with incorruptibility and immortality (1 Cor. 15:53, 54).

Index of Greek Words

This is an index of the transliterated Greek words used within the text of this book. Words are listed according to the order of the English alphabet.

Greek	English	Scripture	Page
a–	without (privative prefix)		155, 159
adiáleipton	unceasingly, without intermission (adjective)	2 Tim. 1:3	131
adialeíptōs	without ceasing (adverb)	1 Thess. 5:17	131
ádolon	unadultered		154, 156
ádolos	without deceit	1 Pet. 2:2	155
agápē	love	Col. 3:14	120
agathón	communicable good	Phile. 1:6	140
agathós	benevolent	Col. 1:10	114
agathosúnē	goodness	Gal. 5:22	119
agnoéō	to ignore		21
agṓn	contention, struggle	1 Thess. 2:2; Heb. 12:1	122, 144
aiṓnios	eternal, timelessness		95
akatharsía	uncleanness	Gal. 5:19	74, 122
akoúō	to hear, obey	John 18:37	56
allássō	to change		101, 115,

Index of Greek Words

allḗlōn	of one another	Col. 3:13	119
állos	another of the same kind		119
amárantos	unfading	1 Pet. 1:4	152
amphí	around		7
amphíblēstron	fishing net (thrown over the shoulder)	Matt. 4:18	7
aná	again		145
anadeíknumi	to show by raising high or aloft	Luke 10:1	29
anádeixis	showing, public propulsion	Luke 1:80	29
anagennáō	to give new birth to		152
anagennḗsas	has regenerated, given new birth to	1 Pet. 1:3	152
anagénnēsis	new birth		152
anechómenoi	forbearing, tolerating	Col. 3:13	119
ánō	up		145
anorthṓsate	to lift up, straighten, strengthen	Heb. 12:12	145
ánthrōpos	man	John 2:25; 3:1	48
anupokrítou	unfeigned, without hypocrisy	2 Tim. 1:5	132
aorgēsía	not showing anger when justified		119
apantáō	to encounter, meet		33

Index of Greek Words

apántēsis	encounter, meeting	1 Thess. 4:17	33
aparchḗ	firstfruits, one making a start	1 Cor. 15:20; Rom. 8:23	99, 163
apekdúō	to put away from		117
apekdusámenoi see *apekdúō*		Col. 3:9	117
áphesis	deliverance from sin		30
aphíemi	to forgive, put away from		120
aphilárguros	without covetousness, without love of money	Heb. 13:5	150
áphthartos	incorruptible	1 Pet. 1:4	152
apó	from		101, 116, 156, 161
apokatallássō	to reconcile	Eph. 2:26; Col. 1:20, 21	101, 116
apóstoloi	apostles	2 Cor. 11:5	108
apothémenoi	laying aside	1 Pet. 2:1	156
apothésthe see *apotíthēmi*		Col. 3:8	117
apotíthēmi	to put away from oneself	(see text for references)	117, 156
arésai	to please (aorist infinitive of *aréskō*)	Rom. 8:8	76
aréskeia	desire of pleasing	Col. 1:10	114
areskeían see *aréskein*		1 Thess. 4:1	114
aréskein	pleasing		76
aréskō	to please		76

167

Index of Greek Words

ártios	perfection, faultlessness	2 Tim. 3:17	88
asebeís	ungodly	Rom. 5:6	65
asélgeia	lasciviousness	Gal. 5:19	74
autó	the same		87
autón	his	Matt. 13:4	3
auxánō	to grow, to give increase	1 Cor. 3:6	28, 92
bállō	to cast, throw		7
basileía	kingdom	John 18:36	55
chalepoí	perilous	2 Tim. 3:1	134
cháris	grace	Rom. 5:2	66, 68, 104, 129, 1152, 161
chárisma	free gift, undeserved benefit	Rom. 5:5	66, 104
charitóō	active pity		152
charizómenoi	providing grace, forgiving	Col. 3:13	120
chrestótēs	kindness, gentleness	Col. 3:12	119
deiloí	timid, fearful	Mark 4:40	11
deḗseis	supplications	1 Tim. 2:1	128, 131
déēsis	supplication		128
délear	bait		123, 155
dḗmos	people		48
désmios	prisoner	Acts 23:18; 28:17; Eph. 3:1; 4:1; 2 Tim. 1:8	148
diá	through (intensive)		11, 68, 115, 121

Index of Greek Words

diakríseis	discernings	1 Cor. 12:10	8
dialássō	to reconcile, change	Matt. 5:24	115
dialégomai see *dielégeto*			121
dialogismós	thought, reasoning	Luke 9:47	22
diánoian	thorough understanding	1 John 5:20	142
dichostasía	dissension		75
dichostasíai	seditions (plural of *dichostasia*)	Gal. 5:20	75
didáskale	teacher	Mark 4:38	11
diegeírō	to arise		11
diegertheís	he arose (passive participle)	Mark 4:39	11
diegeírousin	they awake him	Mark 4:38	11
dielégeto	reasoned	Acts 17:2	121
dielogízesthe	disputed, figured out in one's mind	Mark 9:33	21
dikaióō	to justify		61
dikaíōsis	justification		61
dikaiōthéntes	being justified	Rom. 5:1	62, 67
díkē	justice, trial, retribution		63
dokéō	to recognize		100
dólō	guile		123
dólon see *dólos*		1 Pet. 2:1	156

Index of Greek Words

dólos	guile, deceit	1 Pet. 2:22	123, 155
dóxa	glory		100
echarísthē	it is given free	Phil. 1:29	104
échē	has continuously	John 3:15	53
échō	to have		68
échthra	hatred		74
échthrai	enmities, hatred (plural of *échthra*)	Gal. 5:20	74
edídou	was giving or bringing forth	Matt. 13:8	4
egéneto	became	John 1:14	19, 43
egḗgertai	to raise himself	1 Cor. 15:4; 1 Cor. 15:20	66, 98
egeírō	to arise		11
egertheís	raised	Rom. 6:9	78
ēgnóoun	understood not	Mark 9:32	21
eidōlolatreía	idolatry	Gal. 5:20	74
eídos	the object of sight		19
eilikrinḗs	sincere	1 Pet. 2:2	155
eimí	to be		161
ek	of (preposition)	2 Cor. 5:18	102
ekdúō	to undress		118
ekrataioúto	waxed strong (imperfect passive of *krataióō*)	Luke 1:80	29
elḗlutha	I came	John 18:37	56
éleos	mercy, inner sympathy, pity	1 Pet. 1:3	118, 151

Index of Greek Words

en	in	(see text for references)	3, 19, 73, 96, 123, 128, 133, 149
ēn	had been (imperfect of eimí)		161
endúō	to dress oneself		118
endúsasthe	to dress yourselves	Col. 3:12	118
enoikéō	to indwell		133
enṓkēsen	dwells in	2 Tim. 1:5	133
enteúxeis	intercessions (plural of *énteuxis*)	1 Tim. 2:1	128
énteuxis	intercession		128
enthusámenoi see *endúo*			118
entugchánō	to make intercession for	Rom. 8:27, 34; 11:2; Heb. 7:25	128
ephobḗthēsan	exceedingly afraid	Mark 4:41	11
epígnōsis	knowledge	Col. 1:10	113
epipotheíte see *epipothḗsate*			154
epipothḗsate	desire (aorist imperative)	1 Pet. 2:2	154
epipothéō	to desire earnestly		154
érchomai	I come		56
erchómenos	to keep coming	Rev. 1:4	162
éreis	variance, strife (plural of *éris*)	Gal. 5:20	75
éris	strife		75
eritheía	rivalry, contention	Gal. 5:20	75

Index of Greek Words

eritheíai	strife, contention (plural of *eritheía*)		75
eschḗkamen	we have (perfect indicative of *echō*)	Rom. 5:2	68
esiṓpōn	they were keeping silent	Mark 9:34	22
eskḗnōsen	dwelt	John 1:14	43
estḗkamen	we stand (perfect indicative of *hístēmi*)	Rom. 5:2	68
esthíō	to eat		37
ḗte katērtisménoi	be perfectly joined together	1 Cor. 1:10	88
eu–	good (prefix)		129
eucharistía	thanksgiving		129
eucharistías	giving of thanks (plural of *eucharistía*)	1 Tim. 2:1	129
euchḗ	a vow or wish		128
eulogēménē	one well-spoken of	Luke 1:28, 42	151
eulogéō	to speak well of		151
eulogētós	blessed, well-spoken of	Eph. 1:3; 1 Pet. 1:3	151
eúxane	grew (imperfect of *auxánō*)	Luke 1:80	28, 29
eúxanen	gave increase	1 Cor. 3:6	29
gála	milk	1 Pet. 2:2	154
gegénnēmai	have been born	John 18:37	56
gennáō	to give birth to		56
ginṓskomen	experiential knowledge	1 John 5:20	142

Index of Greek Words

glōsolaliá	speaking in tongues		86
gnṓme	opinion	1 Cor. 1:10	89
hágioi	unblameable, spotless	Col. 1:22	116
hamartánei	to sin	1 John 3:6	82
hamartánōn see *hamartánei*		1 John 3:6	82
hamártē see *hamartánei*		1 John 2:1	82
hamártēte see *hamartánei*		1 John 2:1	82
hairéseis	heresies, discords (plural of *haíresis*)	Gal 5:20	75
haíresis	discord, dissension		75
harpagēsómetha	shall be caught up	1 Thess. 4:17	39
heautoís	one another, your own selves	Col. 3:13	120,
hēméra	day		94
hḗpios	gentle	1 Thess. 2:7	123
hetéra	qualitatively different		19
héteron	another of different quality		19
hierón	temple, sacred building in its entirety		46
hína	that, so that, for the purpose	John 3:15; 18:37	51, 56
hístēmi	to stand		68

Index of Greek Words

ho	the (definite article, masculine)	(see text for references)	3, 42, 43, 52, 78, 82, 155, 161, 162
homologḗsēs	confess	Rom. 10:9	77
homoú	together		77
huiós	adoption, son	Gal. 4:5	83, 130
huiothesía	becoming a son	Gal. 4:5	83
hupér	on behalf of	1 Tim. 2:1, 2	129
hupērétai	subjects (of an authority)		55
huperlían	super (super-human mind)	2 Cor. 11:5; 12:11	87, 108
hupernikáō	to be more than conquerors	Rom. 8:37	72
hupokríseis	pretensions, hypocrisies	Pet. 2:1	156
hupomonḗ	patience		119
hupóstasis	firm substance	Heb. 11:1	142
iáomai	to heal, make whole		33
kaí	and	Rev. 1:4	161, 162
kainḗ	qualitatively new		102
kainós see *kainḗ*		Rev. 21:1	164
kairoí	times	2 Tim. 3:1	134
kairós	time, season	2 Tim. 4:3	134
kakía	unexternalized bad feelings, constitutional malice	1 Pet. 2:1	156
kakouchéō	to suffer adversity	Heb. 13:3	148

Index of Greek Words

kakouchoúmenoi	tormented	Heb. 11:37	148
karpophoréō	to bring forth fruit	Matt. 13:23; Mark 4:20; Luke 8:15; Col. 1:10	113
katá	forward, against		88, 101, 115
katalaliás	evil speakings, slander	1 Pet. 2:1	156
katallagḗ	reconciliation	Rom. 5:11	70, 101
katallássō	to reconcile	Rom. 5:10; 1 Cor. 7:11; 2 Cor. 5:18–20	101, 115, 116
katalláxantos	did reconcile	2 Cor. 5:18	102
katartízō	to put together in order		88
katharízete	cleanse (imperative)		34
katharízō	to cleanse		33
katharós	pure	1 Pet. 2:2	155
kauchṓmetha	boast, rejoice	Rom. 5:2	69
kausóomai see *kausoúmai*			160
kausoúmai	being burned up, set on fire		160
kausoúmena see *kausoúmai*		2 Pet. 3:10, 12	160
kenḗ	in vain, empty	1 Thess. 2:1	121
kérmata	coins		46
kermatistaí	money-changers	John 2:14	46
kermatízō	to divide into small money		46

Index of Greek Words

koinōnía	fellowship		140
koinós	common		140
koítē	a shared bed		149
krataióō	to make strong		29
krátos	strength, stability, steadfastness		29
krísis	judgment, separation		89
kōmoi	revelings (plural of *kōmos*)	Gal. 5:21	75
kōmos	carousing, merry-making		75
kúrios	absolute master	Col. 1:10	114
laléō	to say, repeat		86
latreía	service	Rom. 12:1	80, 155
légō	to say, speak, tell	1 Cor. 1:10	77, 86, 121
logikḗ	reasonable, logical, well-planned	Rom. 12:1	80
logikón	logical	1 Pet. 2:2	154
logikós	reasonable, spiritual, of the Word	1 Pet. 2:2; Rom. 12:1	155
lógos	reason, word, intelligence	John 1:1	30, 86, 155
lúō	to separate, break apart, melt		190
luthḗsontai	shall melt	2 Pet. 3:10	159
máchesthai	to fight, as in a battle	2 Tim. 2:24	123
makariótēs	blessedness		37

Index of Greek Words

makárioi see *makários*		Matt. 5:3–11	36, 106
makários	blessed		36, 37, 151
makrothumía	long-suffering, endurance	Col. 3:12	119
marturéso	I should bear witness	John 18:37	56
mḗ apólētai	should not perish	John 3:15	52
metá	change of condition		19, 81
metamorphó	to transfigure		18, 19
metamórphōsis	transfiguration		18
metamorphoú-mai see *metamorphó*	middle voice of *metamorphó*	Matt. 17:2; Mark 9:2	18
metamor-phoústhe	transformed	Rom. 12:2	81
metaschematízō	to transfigure outward appearance		19
metánoia	change of mind, repentance		30
méthai	drunkenness (plural of *méthē*)	Gal. 5:20	88
méthē	drunken		75
mimētaí	followers	1 Cor. 4:16; 11:1; 1 Thess. 1:6	108, 109 110
mimētḗs	imitator		108, 109
moicheía	adultery	Gal. 5:19	74
moichoí	adulterers	Heb. 13:4	149
monogenḗs	belonging to the same family	John 1:18	42

Index of Greek Words

morphḗ	form (noun)		19, 81
morphṓ	to form		19
morphóō see *morphṓ*			81
morphoúmai	to be formed	Gal. 4:19	19
mou	my, mine		108, 109
naós	temple, sanctuary		46
nikáō	to win		48
noéō	understanding	Heb. 11:3	141
noús	mind		89
nuní	now	1 Cor. 15:20	97, 98
odúnē	sorrow, birth pangs	Rom. 9:2	131
oídamen	knowledge	1 John 5:20	142
oikeí	dwells	1 Cor. 3:16; 2 Cor. 6:16	133
oikéō	to dwell		133
oikodomḗ	building	1 Cor. 3:9; 2 Cor. 5:1	93
oiktirmós	mercy	Col. 3:12	118
ṓn	the one, which is	John 1:18	43, 161
orgḗ	wrath		100
orgelótēs	being angry without cause		119
orégomai	to desire eagerly or earnestly		100
orthóō	to straighten, strengthen		145
ou	negative particle		55

Index of Greek Words

ouk	negative particle (used before a vowel)		55
oukoún	"art thou?" (interrogative)	John 18:37	55
oún	therefore		55
panēguris	gathering, general assembly	Heb. 12:23	147
pánta	all	1 Pet. 2:1	156
pántes	all, collective individuals	1 Cor. 12:13	96
pará	from		15
parádosis	tradition	Matt. 15:2, 3, 6; Mark 7:3, 5, 8, 9, 13	15
paráklēsis	exhortation, calling near	1 Thess. 2:3	122
paráptōma	transgression, offense	Rom. 5:15	66
parastḗsai	present, surrender	Rom. 12:1	80
parístēmi	present (imperative verb)	Rom. 6:19	80
parousía	coming	2 Pet. 3:4	158
parrēsiázomai	to speak boldly, be frank	1 Thess. 2:2	122
pás	anyone, a totality of individuals	John 3:15	51, 52
pásan see *pánta*		Col. 1:10	114
pásas see *pánta*		1 Pet. 2:1	156
pásin see *pánta*		Heb. 13:4	149

Index of Greek Words

pathḗmata	passions	Rom. 7:5	73
peirasmós	temptation		1
peirázo	to tempt		1
peíra	experience, trial		1
peirṓ	to perforate, pierce through		1
peíthō	to persuade		133
Pentēkostḗ	pentecost, fiftieth		94
pépeismai	I am persuaded	2 Tim. 1:5	133
perí	concerning, in regard to	Eph. 6:18	129
peripateín	walk	1 Thess. 4:1	89
phágetai	shall eat	Luke 14:15	44
phónoi	murders (plural of *phónos*)	Gal. 5:21	88
phónos	murder		76
phrónēma	mind-set		71, 119
phthónoi	envyings (plural of *phthónos*)	Gal. 5:21	75
phthónos	envy, wishing evil on others		75
phthónous	envies	1 Pet. 2:1	156
pisteúōn	believing	John 3:15	52
pneúma	spirit		73
porneía	fornication	Gal. 5:19	74
pórnoi	whoremongers	Heb. 13:4	149
praótēs	meekness	Col. 3:12	119
próphasis	a pretext, excuse, a "cloak"	1 Thess. 2:5	123

Index of Greek Words

Greek	Meaning	Reference	Page
prós	toward (preposition)	2 Pet. 3:10	128
prosagōgḗ	access, a leading to	Rom. 5:2; Eph. 2:18; 3:12	68
proseuchaí	prayers (in general)		131
proseuchḗ	prayer		128
proseuchás	prayers (plural of *proseuchḗ*)	1 Tim. 2:1	128
proskephálaion	pillow	Mark 4:38	9
prṓton pántōn	first of all	1 Tim. 2:1	127
prōtotókōn	first-born	Heb. 12:23	147
psuchḗ	soul		73
rhḗma	word, utterance	Luke 3:2	30
rhoizēdón	with a great noise		160
sarkí	flesh	Rom. 7:5	73
sarkikoí	carnal	1 Cor. 3:1	70
sarkikós see *sarkikoí*		Rom. 7:14	91
sárkinoi	fleshly, corpulent, made of flesh	Rom. 7:14	70
sárx	flesh	Rom. 8:8	73, 74, 91
schḗma	shape, form		19, 81
schísmata	divisions, schisms	1 Cor. 1:10	87
schízō	to rip, rend		87
sōthḗsē	shalt be saved	Rom. 10:9	78
sṓzō	to save, heal, bring to safety		33
speírein	to sow continuously	Matt. 13:3	3

Index of Greek Words

speírō	to sow, scatter		3
speírōn	sowing one	Matt. 13:3	3
spláchna	bowels	Col. 3:12	118
splḗn	spleen		118
stoicheía	physical elements	2 Pet. 3:10	158
summimētaí	be followers together	Phil. 3:17	109
summimētḗs see *summimētaí*			109
sún	together (preposition)		81, 109
sunágontai	gathered themselves together	Mark 6:40	15
sunístēmi	to hold together	Col. 1:17	160
suschēmatízesthe	to conform to the age	Rom. 12:2	81
tapeinophrosúnē	humility	Col. 3:12	119
tapeinós	one who recognizes his true condition		119
tḗ see *tó*	[feminine dative definite article]		73
teleiótēs	divine goal, end		120
téknon	beloved child	1 Tim. 1:2, 18; 2 Tim. 1:2; 2:1	130
témnō	to divide		159
therapeúete	heal (imperative)	Matt. 10:8	34
therapeúō	to heal		33
Theón see *Theós*		John 1:1	42

Index of Greek Words

Theós	God	John 1:18	42, 78
theótēs	Godhead		43
Theoú	God, the Father	2 Cor. 5:18	102, 161
thnētoí	mortal		70
thumoí	bad temper, sudden wrath (plural of *thumós*)	Gal. 5:20	75
thumós	anger		75, 100
tíktō	to give birth to		130
timḗ	honor, esteem		149
tímios	honorable	Heb. 13:4	149
tís ára hoútos estin?	"what manner of man is this?"	Mark 4:41	11
títhēmi	to lay, set, put		156
tṓ see *tó*	[masculine, neuter, dative, definite article]	(see text for references)	3
tó	the (definite article)	(see text for references)	9, 87, 154
tón see *tó*		John 1:1	42
toú see *tó*			3, 102
trópos	conversation, way of life, daily behavior	Heb. 13:5	149
tugchánō	to get, attain		128
upéntēsen	encountered	Luke 17:12	33
xúlon	wood, tree		51
zḗloi	emulations, jealousies	Gal. 5:20	75

Index of Greek Words

zḗlos	jealousy		75
zoḗ	life	Luke 15:13; 16:25; Rom. 6:2; Phil. 1:20	50
zōsan	living	Rom. 12:1	80

Scripture Index

Genesis
1:1	141
1:2	95
2:16–25	42
2:17	65
3:3	65
3:15	44, 65
3:16	36
3:17	39
6:9–17	158
6:9—7:10	158
ch. 15—18	58
15:6	58
17:7	58
17:17	58
18:3	148
19:2	148
ch. 22	58
ch. 31	32

Exodus
20:1	16
20:12	17
23:16	94
33:11	42

Leviticus
14:1–32	34
23:9–21	94

Numbers
12:8	42
21:8, 9	50

Deuteronomy
29:29	143

Joshua
ch. 7	32

1 Samuel
15:9	32

2 Samuel
11:1–5	32

1 Kings
19:4	145

2 Kings
5:20	32

Job
26:13	95

Psalms
10:2	57
23:4	2
46:1	152
50:3	160
66:18	126
73:6	57
97:5	160
103:12	60

Proverbs
1:20	142
11:2	57
16:18	57
21:4	57

Scripture Index

Isaiah
55:10, 11	4
1:18	67
32:15	95
40:31	144
66:15, 16	160
53:4	163

Jeremiah
5:31	134, 135

Ezekiel
20:47, 48	160

Daniel
7:7, 8, 21, 25	40
9:25–27	40
9:27	40
12:1	40
12:11	40

Joel
2:30	160

Micah
2:2	31

Zephaniah
1:18	160
3:8	160

Zechariah
9:9, 10	26

Malachi
4:1	160

Matthew
1:18, 20	95
1:21	6, 26
3:4	30
3:16	95
3:16, 17	30
4:17	24
4:18	7
5:1–11	36
5:3	37
5:4	36
5:8	35
5:10	37
5:11	36, 151
5:13–16	39
5:24	115
5:28, 29	22
5:44	145
5:45	104
6:2, 5, 16	16
6:33	2
8:2, 3	33
8:17	163
8:19–26	9
8:28	134
10:8	34
10:14	56
10:34–37	111
11:4, 5	34
11:25	18
13:3	3
13:4	3
13:5	3
13:7	4
13:19	3
13:20	3
13:21	3
13:22	4
13:23	4, 113
14:3	156

Scripture Index

15:2	6, 15	3:5	100, 119
15:3	6, 15	4:20	113
15:3, 6	16	4:26–29	4
15:6	6, 15	4:35	9, 10
15:19	75	4:36	9
16:18, 19	124	4:38	11
17:1	18	4:39	11
17:2	18	4:40	11
17:5	56	4:41	11
18:11	26	5:2	33
18:15	56, 124	6:11	56
18:18	124	6:30	15
19:5	110	6:45, 46	12
19:23, 24	5	6:46	18
20:20–28	12	7:1	15
21:1–11	24	7:2, 3	15
22:37, 38	17	7:3	15
22:37–40	16	7:3–13	6
22:39	17	7:5	15
23:13–15	16	7:6	15, 16
23:37–39	107	7:8	15, 17
24:15	40	7:9	15, 16
24:21	40, 111	7:9–13	17
24:21, 22	163	7:13	15
24:29	40	7:21	75
24:29–35	40	8:32	21
24:30	40	9:2	18
25:14–30	79	9:32	21
25:27	4	9:33	21
25:31–36	24	9:34	22
27:11	55	9:35	22
27:18	75	9:37	23
28:9	33	10:35–45	12
28:18	56	11:1–11	24
		13:14	40
		13:24	40
Mark		13:26	40
1:6	30	13:31	40
1:10	95	14:13	33
1:15	5	14:61	151
1:17	7	15:2	55
1:35	18	15:10	75
1:42	33	16:12	19

187

Scripture Index

Luke

1:11, 12	13
1:28	152
1:28, 42	151
1:30	13
1:35	95
1:68	151
1:80	28, 29
2:10	13, 36
2:40	29
2:41	45
2:42	45
3:1, 2	27
3:2	27, 28, 30
3:3	30
3:21	18
3:22	95
4:27	33
5:16	18
6:12	18
6:20	37
6:21	132
6:22	36
7:11–16	25
7:22	34
8:15	113
8:19–25	9
8:49–55	25
9:18	18
9:28–36	19
9:29	19
9:46	22
9:47	22
10:1	29
10:16	56
11:7	149
12:13–21	5
12:15	31
13:34, 35	107
14:1	37
14:15	37
15:11–32	100
15:13	50
16:25	50
17:14, 17	33
17:17	34
17:20, 21	12, 38
17:20–24	24
17:24	24
18:18–23	5
19:8	140
19:11–27	79
19:28–40	24
21:25	40
21:25, 26	40
21:26	40
21:27	40
21:28	41
21:34	75
22:32	128
23:2	54
23:3	55
23:34	128

John

1:1	30, 42, 62, 78, 95, 142, 155
1:1–5	63
1:3	13
1:4	62
1:10–14	95
1:11	25
1:11, 12	6
1:12	66, 70
1:14	43, 73, 142
1:18	42
1:29	25
2:12	45
2:14	46
2:19	78, 98
2:19–22	50
2:21	46
2:24	48

2:25	48	16:33	37, 105, 147
ch. 3	50	17:1	18
3:1	48	17:21, 23	148
3:3	49, 56, 77, 116	18:13–24	27
3:3–8	61	18:31	54
3:6	49	18:34	55
3:10	49	18:34–38	54
3:15	50-52, 6	18:36	55
3:16	100, 143, 152	18:36, 37	55
3:17	56	18:37	55, 56
3:18	67, 102, 103	18:38	55
3:34	56	19:39	49
4:24	42, 126	20:22, 23	124
4:50	51		
5:24	56	**Acts**	
5:36, 38	56	1:5, 8	96
6:15	12, 54	2:1	94
6:29	56	2:1–13	95, 96
7:37–39	95, 96	2:38	115
7:39	95	4:10	51
8:28	51	4:10, 12	163
8:56	59, 63	4:12	63
8:58	63	5:1–10	124
10:17	78	5:1–11	32
10:17, 18	98	5:41	149
10:28	78, 124, 143	7:58	156
10:33	54	8:24	124
11:38–44	25	8:33	51
11:41	18	9:27, 29	122
12:12–19	24	10:44–46	95
12:27	25	11:14–18	95
12:32	51	13:15	122
12:37	55	13:30	65
14:13, 14	68	13:45	75
14:16, 17	95	13:46	122
15:11	36	14:2–5	105
15:16	68	14:3	122
15:18–21	144	14:19–22	105
16:7–15	95	15:6	124
16:8	77	15:30	122
16:13	96	16:1	132
16:23, 24	68	16:19–40	105
16:24	127		

16:31	63, 147	4:1–3	63
17:1	121	4:2	57
17:2	121	4:3	58, 59
17:3	122	4:4	49
17:4	122	4:5	59, 63
17:5	122	4:5, 6	61
17:17	121	4:6	59
17:25	51	4:6–8	60
18:4	121	4:7	61
18:19	121	4:8	59, 61
18:26	122	4:9	63
19:1–7	95	4:15	62, 146
19:8	122	4:16	63
20:4	138	4:24	63
20:7, 9	121	4:25	75
20:16	94	5:1	60, 61, 63, 64, 67, 70, 116, 161
20:19, 31	132		
20:37	132	5:2	68
22:17–21	126	5:6	65
23:18	148	5:8	152
24:25	121	5:9	70
26:18	70	5:10	70, 79, 100, 101, 115
28:17	148		
		5:11	60, 70, 101
Romans		5:12	39, 100, 104
1:1	83	5:12–14	115
1:11	154	5:13	62
1:16	63	5:15	60, 66
1:21	142	5:17–19	60
1:24	74, 123	5:18, 19	60
1:25	151	5:21	60
1:29	75	6:2	51
2:8	75	6:6	71, 80, 91, 117
2:12	62	6:9	78
2:15	62	6:11	117
3:20	57, 62, 146	6:12	79
3:21	62, 98	6:14	80
3:22	63	6:17, 20	82
3:23	65, 100	6:18, 19	63
3:26	60	6:19	80, 123
3:27, 28, 31	62	6:22	98
4:1	57	ch. 7	71, 118
		7:5	73

Scripture Index

7:6	57	ch. 9—11	79
7:7–9	58	9:2	131
7:14	70, 91	9:3	124
7:14–25	71	9:5	151
7:15	71	9:33	63
7:17	71	10:4	62, 63
7:18	74	10:9	52, 65, 77, 78
7:18–21	71	10:9–11	63
7:23	61	10:10	77
7:25	71	10:12	77, 141
8:1	73, 74	10:13	77
8:3	60, 62, 64, 73	11:2	128
8:4	73, 74	11:15	101
8:5	73, 74	ch. 12	79
8:5–9	71	12:1	80, 155
8:7	71, 76	12:2	18, 81
8:8	73, 74, 76	12:5	90
8:11	66, 70, 78, 133	12:13	148
8:12	71	13:1–3	129
8:13	71	13:12	156
8:14	126	13:13	75, 149
8:15	143	ch. 14	83
8:15–17	116	14:1	83
8:17	10	14:2–6	83
8:19–23	116	14:7–9	83
8:20	39	14:10	147
8:20–22	71	14:10–13	84
8:20–23	39	14:13	89
8:21	39	14:21	83
8:21, 22	40, 163	16:17	124
8:22	143		
8:23	39, 41, 70, 79, 112, 143, 144, 153, 163	**1 Corinthians**	
		1:5	141
8:24	152	1:10	86, 92
8:26	68, 126	1:11	75
8:27	128	1:12–14	88
8:28	143	1:13	91
8:33	61	1:13–17	88, 91
8:33, 34	60	1:20	141
8:34	78, 128	1:23	5
8:37	72	1:25, 27	6
8:38, 39	143	1:30	60, 63, 90

2:1	92	12:26	116, 148
2:7–16	159	13:8	5
2:9–12	143	13:9	86
2:14	49	14:1–16	126
2:16	89	15:1–4	56, 87
3:1	70, 90, 92	15:2	87
3:2	90	15:3	64
3:3	75	15:3–9	97
3:6	27, 92	15:4	66
3:9	93	15:4–8	142
3:10–12	7	15:12	66, 97
3:10–15	7	15:12–19	97
3:11–15	136	15:13	66
3:16	133	15:14	78, 142
ch. 4	110	15:17	142
4:6	19	15:18	142
4:16	108, 109	15:20	66, 78, 97–99
5:2	124	15:20, 23	163
5:5	124	15:23	94
5:7	45	15:24–28	26
5:11	98, 124, 125	15:36, 42–49	99
5:13	124	15:50	38
6:11	52	15:51	99
6:14	66	15:52	116, 152
7:3–5	149	15:52–54	39, 153
7:11	101	15:53, 54	70, 79, 164
7:26–35	149	16:1–4	138
9:12	105	16:8	94
9:25	152	16:13	29
10:14	74	16:22	124
11:1	108-110		
11:2	110		

2 Corinthians

11:3	110
11:19	75	1:3	151
11:20–29	110	1:6	105
chs. 12—14	86	2:4	132
12:1	92	2:5–10	125
12:1–31	116	3:18	18
12:4–11	96	4:11	70, 79
12:10	8	4:16	144
12:11	4	5:1	93, 143
12:12–23	88	5:2	154
12:13	51, 52, 61, 90, 96	5:4	79

5:10	147	5:21	75
5:15	25	5:22	4, 119
5:17	25, 61, 91, 101, 116, 143	5:22, 23	114
		6:1	125
5:18	79, 101, 102, 115	6:2	116, 148
5:18–20	101, 115	6:9	144
5:19–21	60		
5:21	25, 50, 60, 63, 64	## Ephesians	
		1:3	151
6:16	133	1:4	62
6:17	74	1:6	152
9:14	154	1:13	39
11:5	87, 108	1:13, 14	153
11:13–15	19	1:13–19	63
11:21–33	110	1:16–18	126
11:24	111	1:17	78
11:31	151	1:19, 20	98
12:11	87	1:22	116
12:20	75	2:1	57, 69
12:21	123	2:2	1, 3
		2:2, 3	82
## Galatians		2:5–8	51
1:1	98	2:6	69
1:4	64, 78	2:8	77, 161
1:8	124	2:12	152
2:11	124	2:15, 16	74
2:16	62	2:16	101, 115
2:20	60, 71, 80	2:18	68
2:21	62	3:1	148
3:6	58	3:12	79
3:6, 8	63	3:16	29
3:11	62	4:1	148
3:13	60, 146	4:4–6	92
3:18, 21, 23	62	4:11, 12	96
3:24	62, 146	4:15	116
3:28	51	4:19	74, 123
4:5	62	4:22, 25	156
4:5–7	83	4:31	157
4:19	19	5:1	108
5:16	73	5:3	123
5:19	123	5:23	116
5:19–21	74, 114, 157	6:14	63

6:18	126, 128, 129	1:20, 21	101, 116
6:19	129	1:21	100
6:20	122	1:22	116
6:21, 22	138	2:9	11, 13, 20
		2:12	69

Philippians

		3:1	69
1:1	83	3:2	118, 150
1:6	60	3:3	117
1:8	154	3:5	31, 118, 150
1:11	63	3:8	156, 157
1:12	111	3:8, 9	117, 118
1:15	75	3:9	117, 118
1:17	75	3:10	118
1:20	51	3:12	118, 119
1:21	61, 67, 130	3:13	119, 120
1:29	104, 105	3:14	120
2:3	75	3:16	133
2:6, 7	19	4:7–9	138
2:12	113	4:9	137
2:26	154	4:12	139
2:29	111	4:13	139
3:1	151		
3:1, 8	145	## 1 Thessalonians	
3:9	63	1:2, 3	126
3:10	104, 111	1:6	108, 110
3:17	108, 109, 111	1:10	111, 158
3:18	111	2:1	121
3:19	112	2:2	105, 122
3:20, 21	112	2:3	122
3:21	219, 39	2:4	123
4:3	147	2:5	123
4:6	145	2:6	123
		2:7	123

Colossians

		2:8	123
1:7	139	2:10	121
1:9	113	2:14	105, 108, 111
1:10	113, 114	3:6	154
1:13	52, 70	4:1	76
1:16	160	4:7	74, 123
1:17	160	4:13–17	163
1:18	152	4:13–18	39
1:20	116	4:15–17	111

4:17	33, 158	1:5	132, 133
5:4, 5	70	1:8	148
5:14	124	1:14	133
5:17	131	2:1	130, 133
		2:24	123
		3:1	134

2 Thessalonians

1:4, 5	105	3:1–5	39
1:6–12	40	3:10–12	144
1:7	111	3:11	132
1:7–10	26	3:12	105
2:2, 3	125	3:16	159
2:3	40	3:17	88
2:3, 4	40	4:3	134
3:6	124	4:6–8	130
3:8	125		
3:10	125		

Titus

3:11	125
3:13	125

1:6	123
1:8	148
2:13	39

1 Timothy

1:2	130, 132, 159	3:3	75
1:11	151	3:9	75
1:18	130, 133	3:12	132
1:18–20	127, 128		

Philemon

2:1	128	1:1	139
2:1, 2	129	1:2	140
2:2	129	1:4, 5	140
2:4	129	1:6	140
3:2	123, 148	1:7	140
4:5	128	1:8	140
4:8	51	1:9	140
5:20	124	1:9, 10	137
6:4	75	1:10	138, 140
6:10	31, 32	1:11	98
		1:11, 12	140
		1:13	138, 140

2 Timothy

1:1	130	1:14	140
1:2	130, 133	1:15	140
1:3	131	1:16	137
1:4	132, 154	1:18	140
		1:23	139

Hebrews

2:9	106
2:10	106
4:15	10
5:8	106
5:14	8
6:4–6	53
6:12	108
7:25	91, 128
9:14	95
9:14, 22	147
9:26	62
9:27	136
9:28	64
10:14	60
10:32, 33	106
10:32–34	144
11:1	142
11:3	141
11:6	143
11:9	141
11:10	147
11:11	141
11:16	147
11:25	106
11:37	148
12:1	144, 145, 156
12:12	144, 145
12:14, 15	145
12:15	144
12:18	146
12:19	146
12:20	146
12:21	146
12:22	146
12:23	147
12:24	147
13:1	148
13:2	148
13:3	148
13:4	149
13:5	149
13:14	147

James

1:2	2, 145
1:2–4	111
1:21	156
2:14–26	62, 113
2:23	58
3:14, 16	75
4:4	74, 100
4:5	75
4:14	51
5:10	106
5:16	124

1 Peter

1:3	79, 151, 152, 152
1:4	152
1:5	153
1:6, 7	153
1:9	153
1:11	106
1:23	152
2:1	75, 156, 157
2:2	154–56
2:9	52, 70
2:19, 20	105
2:20	106
2:22	123
2:24	64, 163
3:14	106
3:14, 17	105
3:17	106
3:18	60, 64
3:19–21	62
4:1	64
4:3	75
4:9	148
4:12–16	144
4:16	105, 106
4:19	106
5:10	105, 106

2 Peter

1:4	118
1:19	39
2:1	75
2:5, 6	158
2:15	32
2:19	82
3:3	158
3:4	158
3:5, 6	158
3:7	158
3:10	158, 160
3:12	158, 160
3:13	158

1 John

1:6	70
1:7	34, 147
1:7, 9	64
1:9	60, 70, 77, 124
2:1	82
2:2	6
2:9–11	148
2:29	64
3:2	69, 143
3:6	82
3:10, 16, 17	148
4:10	64
4:12	51
4:20, 21	148
5:14, 15	143
5:20	51, 142

2 John

1:10	124

Jude

1:1	83
1:11	32
1:20	126
1:22, 23	125

Revelation

1:4	161
1:5	64, 162
1:5–7	162
1:10	162
2:10	105
3:5	147
3:17, 18	49
7:1–9	163
7:14	40, 163
7:17	164
9:21	75
11:7	40
13:8	62, 65, 147
13:11	40
17:8	62, 147
20:12, 15	147
21:1	39, 41, 143, 163, 164
21:2	147
21:3	147
21:4	163
21:8	149
21:10	147
22:15	149